KT-399-430

Robert Winston

Evolution Revolution

A DORLING KINDERSLEY BOOK

LONDON, NEW YORK, MUNICH,
MELBOURNE, and DELHI

Senior editors Deborah Lock, Wendy Horobin
Designers Sadie Thomas, Laura Roberts-Jensen,
Claire Patané, Sonia Moore, Vicky Wharton,
Clemence de Molliens, Lauren Rosier,
Clare Shedden, Tory Gordon-Harris

Picture researcher Myriam Mégharbi
Indexer Chris Bernstein
Production editor Sean Daly
Production controller Clare Pearson
Jacket designers Karen Shooter, Natalie Godwin
Jacket editor Mariza O'Keeffe
Publishing manager Bridget Giles
Art director Rachael Foster
Creative director Jane Bull
Publisher Mary Ling

Consultant Kim Dennis-Bryan
Associate Lecturer of Evolution, Open University

First published in Great Britain in 2009 by
Dorling Kindersley Limited
80 Strand, London WC2R 0RL

Copyright © 2009 Dorling Kindersley Limited
A Penguin Company
2 4 6 8 10 9 7 5 3 1
WD186 – 11/08

All rights reserved. No part of this publication may
be reproduced, stored in a retrieval system, or transmitted
in any form or by any means, electronic, mechanical,
photocopying, recording, or otherwise, without the prior
written permission of the copyright owner.

A CIP catalogue record for this book
is available from the British Library.

ISBN: 978-1-40533-719-9

Colour reproduction in UK by Alta Image
Printed and bound by L Rex, China

Discover more at
www.dk.com

"

The theory of evolution has been called the greatest scientific idea of all time. In biology — the study of plants and animals — there is no idea that compares with Charles Darwin's thinking about evolution. Although the basic notion that the many species of animals had developed from earlier creatures was not entirely new, Darwin came to riveting conclusions.

He understood that all living things evolved from more primitive forms of life, deciding this process happened over millions of years of tiny changes. Darwin also explained how this was a gradual response to the environment. If a species of animal or plant could not adapt to hostile circumstances, it and its offspring would eventually die out.

Darwin's ideas aroused wonder, criticism, and fury. More than 150 years later, his ideas are still controversial in some parts of the world. It is not easy to accept that we are descended from apes.

Darwin's ideas have become more convincing with time, the more we study biology. Evolution explains how we came to exist, and how we fit into the world about us. Such knowledge helps us understand disease and health, and our emotions and instincts. Above all, the recognition that we are so close to other living organisms gives us greater respect for all life forms on our amazing planet.

"

ROBERT WINSTON

CONTENTS

Why is there life on Earth? Where do we come from? For **millennia** people have tried to answer these questions. In 1858, *Charles Darwin* unveiled his **theory of natural selection** to explain how **LIFE** evolved on Earth. The following year he finished ON **THE ORIGIN OF SPECIES, a book** that **changed the world.** It challenged the status of *humans* and sparked debates about the development of *species* that continue *today*.

HABITS OF A DIODON   13

the limits of the tidal waves ; and as the rivulet slowly trickles down, the surf must supply the polishing power of the cataracts in the great rivers. In like manner, the rise and fall of the tide probably answer to the periodical inundations ; and thus the same effects are produced under apparently different but really similar circumstances. The origin, however, of these coatings of metallic oxides, which seem as if cemented to the rocks, is not understood ; and no reason, I believe, can be assigned for their thickness remaining the same.

DIODON MACULATUS (DISTENDED AND CONTRACTED).

One day I was amused by watching the habits of the Diodon antennatus, which was caught swimming near the shore. This fish, with its flabby skin, is well known to possess the singular power of distending itself into a nearly spherical form. After having been taken out of water for a short time, and then again immersed in it, a considerable quantity both of water and air is absorbed by the mouth, and perhaps likewise by the branchial orifices. This process is effected by two methods : the air is swallowed, and is then forced into the cavity of the body, its

"Whilst this planet has gone cycling on according to fixed laws of gravity, from so SIMPLE a beginning... endless forms most beautiful and most wonderful, have been, and are being evolved."

– Charles Darwin (1858)

"The war of nature is not incessant, death is generally prompt, and the vigorous, the healthy, and the happy survive and multiply."

– Charles Darwin (1859)

THE SEARCH FOR ANSWERS

Have you ever stopped and taken a moment to watch an insect, peer into a flower, or listen to the birds?

How come everything seems to be so perfectly adapted to its environment?

Have you ever marvelled at how many different types, or species, of creatures and plants there are?

You are not the first to ponder over these observations. People have been wondering and questioning for many hundreds of years. And trying to answer the biggest mystery of all: how were we all made?

Hey, salamander, I hear you were once hot stuff!

Yep, those medieval folk thought I was *"created"* in the *flames of a fire.*

Creation stories

In the flickering light of a campfire, people living long ago tried to explain how animals, plants, and people were created. Around the world, their stories varied, telling of one God or many gods or spirits creating life, and these tales were passed down from generation to generation.

GREEK MYTHS

According to an ancient Greek story, the laurel tree was formed when Daphne, a river nymph who was being chased by the god of love, Apollo, cried out in exhaustion to Gaia, the Mother Earth god. Gaia turned Daphne into the tree.

Daphne becomes a laurel tree.

> Job's done! Time to go back to sleep.

DREAMTIME

Aborigines believe that all forms of life, the Ancestors, lay sleeping underneath the crust of Earth. Awoken when time split apart, they wandered around the Earth calling all living things into being and showing them how to live.

In the beginning...

> *I need some excitement around here.*

BRAHMA

The Hindu god of creation, Brahma, used the lotus flower he had been sitting on in a vast dark ocean to create the world and all living things. To the plants he gave feeling and to all animals he gave the senses of touch and smell, and the power to see, hear, and move.

Lotus flower

PACIFIC TALES

The early people living on some islands in the Pacific Ocean told stories of the first people hatching from eggs laid by a bird-headed god or turtle.

10

THE GARDEN OF EDEN

Genesis, the first book of the Bible, tells of everything being created by God in six days. Each species of animal was independently created, perfectly designed for a specific purpose. Adam and Eve were made in God's likeness, so they were different from animals and given a more important role. In Western Europe, the deep-rooted religious belief in this story influenced scientific thinking for many years.

Skunk

Adam + Noah + Abraham + Jacob + Moses + David + Solomon + ...

I am actually a beautiful girl!

1654

SACRED SPIRITS

A Native American tale tells of a beautiful but vain white-haired girl who one day rudely mocked a strange-looking man. The man revealed himself to be one of the great spirits. In anger, the spirit turned the girl into a skunk. Her beautiful hair became the furry white stripe down her back. She was the first of the species of skunk.

**James Ussher
(1581–1656)**

CREATION DAY

After carefully calculating the ages of people mentioned in the Bible, James Ussher, an Irish Archbishop, believed he knew the exact date of the biblical Creation – Sunday 23 October, 4004 BCE. This made Earth less than 6,000 years old.

The *debate* begins...

> Order! Order! Everything needs to be in order.

THE BIRTH OF THE CLASSIFICATION SYSTEM
The botanist Carl Linnaeus grouped all known living things into categories, arranging them into a "Divine Order of God's creation". He devised a system that divided living things into kingdoms, classes, orders, genera, and species. He gave each plant and animal two Latin names made up of the genus (or group) and the species, which scientists still use today. He classified humans as *Homo sapiens* meaning "wise man".

Carl Linnaeus (1707–1778)

> I abandon everything in my book.

> Sniff, sniff!

Georges-Louis Leclerc (1707–1788)

1735

1749

SPECIES
Homo sapiens

GENUS
Homo

> Linnaeus has grouped us with apes!

FAMILY
Hominidae

> Was that God's intention?

ORDER
Primates

CLASS
Mammalia

KINGDOM
Animalia

BUFFON'S LAWS OF NATURE
The Comte de Buffon, Georges-Louis Leclerc, wrote a 44-volume natural history book series between 1749 and 1804, but only published a few copies. He put forward the idea that all living things had been modified from a single ancestor through natural laws working in the environment or by chance. **Shock horror!** *He was challenging the biblical Genesis story.* Without proof though, he was unable to justify his views, which were seen as against God. Later he was forced to publicly withdraw them.

Botanists and naturalists throughout the 18th century *classified and observed plants and studied vertebrate and invertebrate animals.* Some scientists began to *question and challenge* the popular belief that God had created all species as they appear now. Murmurings about species having evolved began to stir up a heated debate.

A pupil of Buffon, *Chevalier de Lamarck* was the first to confidently and very publicly publish a theory of evolution. *He suggested that living things changed by a process of two forces pulling against each other.*

Lamarck suggested that the changes involved in both forces were due to SUBTLE FLUIDS. These flowed all around the body, producing movement and change. For example, snails have poor sight and Lamarck imagined an ancestral snail with no feelers trying to feel its way about. In doing so, "masses of nervous fluid as well as other liquids" would be sent to the front of the head, which in time would produce extended feelers.

Feelers at last!

Chevalier de Lamarck
(1744–1829)

1809

But Lamarck's thinking could be easily attacked and discredited by critics.

If he were correct about inheriting acquired features then the children of professional weightlifters would be born with bulgy muscles.

LAMARCK'S CHANGING FORCES

Force 1 All living things began as simple organisms and then progressed by changing gradually to become more complex and perfect. Lamarck thought humans had reached perfection. He also suggested that the simple organisms were created continuously by "spontaneous generation" from non-living matter, such as wet straw. (Later, the French microbiologist, Louis Pasteur, boiled some straw but nothing developed.)

Force 2 Animals underwent a bodily change during their lifetime to fit into their environment. These favourable changes were then passed on to their offspring. Changes would be made either by the use or the disuse of a feature. For example, a giraffe's neck would become longer by stretching further to get the leaves in the trees.

Fossil *mysteries*

Since ancient times, the finding of fossils has fascinated people. To begin with people wondered what they were and did they have magical powers. Once people realized that fossils came from dead creatures, questions arose about why so many fossils of sea creatures were found on mountain tops. After finding an answer to this that fitted with the Bible, a further discovery of giant fossils made everyone have to think again.

According to the Bible story, Noah took every animal species on board his ark during the Great Flood.

After the flood, we all had lots of babies.

DILUVIALISM THEORY

Up until the end of the 18th century, diluvialism was a popular theory. The theory goes that Earth's surface was reshaped during the great biblical flood when it rained for 40 days and 40 nights. All fossils were drowned creatures that had been formed at this time. The high waters had carried sea creatures to mountain tops and left them there as the waters went down.

1817

Fossilized teeth of a mosasaur

FOSSILS OF GIANTS

During the 1700s, fossils of giant creatures were being discovered and described, including the mosasaur, a giant marine reptile. People believed that the creatures must still exist since Noah had saved them. But where were they now? They would be so large that even in unexplored areas, these gigantic creatures would be unable to hide themselves.

EXTINCTION IDEA

After studying fossils found in the area around Paris, the naturalist Georges Cuvier concluded that they were thousands of centuries old. His observations increased the age of Earth well beyond the accepted 6,000 years. Cuvier also noted that these fossils did not look like anything still living, so these creatures must now be *extinct*.

Georges Cuvier (1769–1832)

CATASTROPHE THEORY

Much admired for his brilliant mind, Georges Cuvier concluded from his fossil and natural history studies that Earth had been dramatically reshaped by a series of *major catastrophes* – the last one being the biblical flood. In his opinion, other floods, earthquakes, and climate changes had caused the previous catastrophes.

Cuvier's wrong and I'm right! The watermarks on these ruined pillars prove that in the last 2,000 years, the land has dropped below sea level and then slowly been pushed up again.

ROCK OF AGES

Fascinated by rocks, the geologist Charles Lyell had a totally opposing view to Cuvier's catastrophe theory. He proposed that the reshaping of Earth in the past had been formed by the same *gradual changes* as can be seen now. For the first page of his book *The Principles of Geology*, Lyell chose an engraving of the ancient temple of Serapis.

Charles Lyell (1797–1875)

The ancient temple of Serapis.

1830 1831

REBUILDING GIANTS

At the Natural History Museum in Paris, Cuvier became famous for being able to construct a complete animal from just a few fossil bones. One of his most famous reconstructions was the giant elephant-like creature called the mastodon. Cuvier was surprisingly accurate.

TRIP OF A LIFETIME

In 1831, a young naturalist, Charles Darwin, joined a survey ship HMS *Beagle* on a five-year voyage around the world. He took with him Lyell's book and, throughout the voyage, he saw rock formations and experienced earthquakes that convinced him Lyell was right about the land slowly reshaping.

15

Hmmm...some people won't like my idea. I won't publish until my idea is fool-proof!

Revolution!

Darwin's idea of *evolution* slowly

dawned on him after returning from his voyage. But he knew from *Lamarck's* and others' experiences that he would not be taken seriously without sound evidence. So he set about researching. It was a further **20 years** before Darwin announced his THEORY OF NATURAL SELECTION, which would send shockwaves across the scientific community.

Darwin's *big* idea

To work, natural selection needs three things:

① VARIATION

All individuals within a species have different characteristics, or *variations*. More individuals are born than will survive to adulthood.

> WE'RE ALL SLIGHTLY DIFFERENT, BUT I HAVE THE **BIGGEST** EARS AND THE **THICKEST** FUR. SO I CAN HEAR AND STAY WARM THE BEST.

1859

1860

PUBLISHED

ON THE ORIGIN OF SPECIES, published in 1859, was an "abstract", or summary, of Darwin's theory of how living things had evolved, which he proposed was through a process he called "*natural selection*".
He intended to write a more detailed book later but never did.

THE ORIGIN OF SPECIES

OUTRAGE!

Seven months later, the British Association held a meeting of well-respected scientists and philosphers inside the Oxford University Museum to debate whether natural things had evolved. Most vocal for the *"Yes, they did!"* view was the biologist, Thomas Huxley, and for the *"No, they didn't!"* view was Bishop Samuel Wilberforce. The meeting ended in uproar.

WILBERFORCE

HUXLEY

ARTIFICIAL SELECTION

The greyhound has been bred to have great eyesight and amazing running speed.

Darwin learned much from breeders of plants and animals, who saw the small variations between individuals. A dog breeder would choose a desired feature and mate two dogs with that feature. The puppies with this chosen feature would be picked out and bred. Over many generations, the feature would become more obvious. Darwin realized a similar process was happening in the wild.

② COMPETITION

With so many individuals competing against each other, the slight variations among them give some a better chance of survival than others in their environment.

WHO SURVIVES? *Nature* DECIDES!

③ INHERITANCE

Because they are more successful, some variations occur more often than others. Over many generations, a noticeable modification, or adaptation, might be seen. Over time, these changes could result in a *new species.*

DARWIN PUBLISHED MORE BOOKS.

1871   1872   1880

Darwin continued to publish books, applying his thinking about how natural selection worked. In **THE DESCENT OF MAN**, Darwin argued that humans shared a common ancestor with apes.

THE LONDON SKETCH BOOK.

PROF. DARWIN.

Darwin sparked scientists' interest in animal behaviour when he stated that there were links between the way animals and humans expressed emotion in **THE EXPRESSION OF THE EMOTIONS IN MAN AND ANIMALS**.

In **THE POWER OF MOVEMENT IN PLANTS**, Darwin explained how climbing plants had evolved their ability to grow upwards to get more sunlight.

DARWIN AND HIS THEORY

Can you imagine yourself working in secret on a brilliant idea you've had for over 20 years, not letting anyone know except a couple of close friends? That's just what Charles Darwin did, and the hard work was worth it!

Chas dear, you spend more time with your plants and specimens than with me!

When he eventually published his theory of natural selection, supported by a hefty load of evidence, Darwin became internationally famous.

Even 150 years later his work is still being mentioned in books like this one.

Big *adventure*

The Captain, **Robert FitzRoy**, nearly prevented Darwin joining the voyage because he didn't like the shape of his nose!

On completing his exams, Darwin returned home uncertain of his future. Awaiting him there was a letter that would change his life. It was from John Henslow, who had turned down an opportunity to be the naturalist on board the survey ship HMS *Beagle*, which was to sail around the world. He had recommended that Darwin should go in his place.

The HMS *Beagle* set out with a crew of 73 men.

Around the World ticket
Admit one Adult.
Position: Voyager - Naturalist, H.M.S. Beagle

AROUND THE WORLD

The HMS *Beagle* set sail from England in December 1831 and finally returned home five years later in October 1836.

Darwin's telescope

GENERAL CHART shewing the PRINCIPAL TRACKS of H.M.S. BEAGLE _ 1831-6.

1835

1832

Start voyage: England 1831

End voyage: England 1836

1833-1834

1836

1836

——— = Journey to Galápagos
——— = Journey back to England

Galápagos Islands

Abingdon I.
Tower I.
Bindloes I.
Narborough I.
James I.
Indefatigable I.
Albemarle I.
Barrington I.
Chatham I.
Charles I.
Hood's I.

CURIOUS ISLES

After nearly four years surveying the coastline of South America, the HMS *Beagle* sailed to the nearby cluster of black-lava rock islands of the Galápagos. On his island excursions, Darwin collected many rocks and plants, and used his hunting skills to capture animals, particularly birds, to take back to England.

Darwin saw the world's largest variety of tortoise on the Galápagos. Local people told him that they knew which island a tortoise had come from just by looking at its shell.

BEAK MYSTERY

Darwin was fascinated by the different beak shapes of the birds he saw. He did not realize until after he had returned home that the 13 species he collected were all finches. He would later conclude that the finches had evolved from a shared ancestor and each species had developed different beaks to adapt to eating different foods for survival.

The "swarms" of marine iguanas lying on the rocks horrified the crew. They are the only iguanas that swim in the sea to feed. They return to the rocks to warm up.

Marine iguana

MAKING WAVES

In August 1839, Darwin published his diary of the *Beagle* voyage. This book summarized his findings and insights about the local and colonial people he met. It was well received and he established himself as a popular author.

WEIRD AND WONDERFUL

Darwin collected thousands of specimens during the voyage. He and his assistant, Syms Covington, stopped them decaying by either removing their innards and stuffing them with cotton, or placing them in jars of wine and sealing tightly. Once home, he sent many of the specimens to various botanists and naturalists, who made detailed drawings of them.

A parrotfish caught by Darwin and preserved in wine.

Darwin's scorpion fish drawn by Leonard Jenyns, naturalist

JOURNAL OF RESEARCHES
INTO THE
NATURAL HISTORY & GEOLOGY
OF THE
COUNTRIES VISITED DURING THE VOYAGE ROUND
THE WORLD OF H.M.S. 'BEAGLE'
UNDER THE COMMAND OF CAPTAIN FITZ ROY, R.N.

BY CHARLES DARWIN, M.A., F.R.S.

LONDON
JOHN MURRAY, ALBEMARLE STREET
1890

UPS and *downs*

Hurray! Darwin's finally home.

Loved your letters! More! More!

On his return to England, Darwin found himself already a scientific *celebrity*. Henslow had distributed a few of Darwin's letters from his voyage among scientists, who had been IMPRESSED. Enthusiastically Darwin started the huge task of organizing his notes and cataloguing all the specimens he had collected, but a mysterious illness was to slow him down.

Letter for Darwin!

Puzzling illness

Shortly after returning from his voyage, Darwin began to suffer from violent sickness, severe pain, and dizziness. Doctors, including his father, were unable to identify the cause and could not suggest a cure. Had he been bitten by some strange creature while on his voyage? This mysterious illness occurred frequently throughout the rest of his life, which meant that Darwin was forced to stay at home.

DOWN HOUSE

Married life

After making a list of the advantages and disadvantages of marrying, Darwin concluded that this would be a good idea. He married his cousin, Emma Wedgwood. She was nicknamed "little Miss Slip-Slop" because of her untidiness, but that didn't bother Darwin. Just before the birth of their third child, the family moved from London to a large house and gardens, called Down House, in easy reach of London. Here, Darwin lived happily with Emma and his ten children.

"Write a letter, write a letter,
Good advice will make us better."

A man of letters

Stuck at home, Darwin kept in touch with people through letters. Darwin corresponded with over 2,000 people during his lifetime. They were not just scientists, but also gardeners, gamekeepers, animal and plant breeders, and those travelling or located abroad. Darwin received over 14,000 letters and probably wrote more than 7,000.

Secret notebooks

In July 1837, Darwin had the beginnings of an idea that he knew would spark a **HUGE** debate about the *religious thinking* of the time. He began *scribbling* his thoughts into the first of many notebooks, which he would *keep secret*.

He sketched a branching tree to show a family history for animals where they shared a common ancestor. He believed that species had changed over time. But what process had made this happen? Darwin knew his idea had to be supported and set about gathering evidence and experimenting.

A bat's wing is supported by elongated finger bones.

Bones in common

All mammals share the same basic patterns of limb bones. These similarities suggest that they share a common ancestor.

BAT WING

WOLF PAW

PORPOISE FLIPPER

Darwin only shared his thoughts on evolution with two of his closest friends. Charles Lyell was an expert on rock formations and Joseph Hooker was an expert on plants.

Naturalist at work

Darwin's microscope

Every day, Darwin spent many hours in his study or his garden experimenting, observing, and analyzing plants, animals, and rocks. He filled his secret notebooks with any evidence of species evolving. In 1844, he wrote a 189-page manuscript outlining his evolutionary theory, but he still didn't publish and continued to collect evidence.

A drawer containing some of Darwin's specimens

Darwin collected 1,529 species

KITCHEN GARDEN

The garden of Down House became a laboratory – a place for investigating and experimenting. Within the large walled vegetable and flower garden, Darwin built his greenhouse, where he set up many experiments to understand the pollination, fertilization, and adaptability of plants.

> Buzz! I fancy that bee over there. I've been fooled, *it's only an orchid!*

DAILY ROUTINE: Walk before breakfast; 08:00 Work in study; 09:30 Read letters; 10:30 Work; 12:00 Walk;

FANCY PIGEONS

Darwin bought many breeds of domestic pigeons and became convinced through analyzing their features that they were all descended from the rock dove. The pigeons showed him how much variation in colour, shape, feathers, and bone structure existed in a single type of animal.

The skeleton of a pigeon, bred, examined, and labelled by Darwin as part of his research on evolution.

Skeleton of a mouse

A FAMILY VENTURE

On occasions, members of the household were involved in collecting information for Darwin. His children tracked the flight patterns of bumblebees and noted the locations of spider webs. Even their governess joined them in counting plant species in a meadow. Servants would help him boil carcasses of small mice and birds so that their skeletons could be studied.

FOSSIL FINDINGS

In South America, Darwin found remains of a giant armoured animal, a glyptodon, which he realized looked similar to the smaller armadillos he saw. Was this evidence of a species that had evolved?

Glyptodon

Armadillo

UNDER THE MICROSCOPE

Darwin wanted to establish himself as an expert on one particular species and chose the subject of barnacles.

Barnacles

Darwin became fascinated by them and became deeply involved in the subject for eight years. He was sent a huge number of barnacles and fossils of barnacles and was able to see how there were many species and that they were all related to each other.

DARWIN'S RHEA

Darwin came across a rare species of rhea in part of South America. This was different from the more common rhea in that area. Had the two species a common ancestor?

Darwin's rhea

and 3,907 other specimens on his voyage.

GREENHOUSE LAB

Darwin was fascinated by the shape of an orchid and after numerous tests he was convinced that these flowers and the insects that pollinated them had evolved together to become perfectly adapted.

The lower petals of the bee orchid have evolved to look like a bee, fooling male bees to visit and pollinate the flower.

13:00 Lunch; 13:30 Work; 15:00 Rest; 16:00 Walk; 16:30 Work; 17:30 Rest; 19:30 Tea; 20:00 Family games; 22:30 Bed.

NOW TRY THIS!

Make a collection box using a shoebox, some little boxes, cardboard, and a shoelace.

1 Decorate your shoebox

Matchboxes

2 Cut out three pieces of cardboard to fit inside the shoebox.

3 Make a hole in the cardboard and thread a loop of shoelace through it. Now glue the boxes onto the cardboard to make your collecting trays.

4 Fill the shoebox with the finished trays and start your collection!

5 If something is too big, use scissors to cut down the sides of two connecting matchboxes to make a larger compartment.

SELECT THE BEST

Darwin's theory that species in the wild had evolved through a process of **NATURAL SELECTION** had its roots in understanding that for many thousands of years, *people had been very selective in developing plants by collecting seeds only from those* PLANTS WITH THE PREFERRED FEATURE. The great variety of different-looking vegetables within the cabbage family was an obvious example to Darwin.

Leafy buds

In Belgium, growers were selecting cabbages with tightly packed leafy buds along the main stem. Over time, the plants began producing more and more of these buds and BY THE 18TH CENTURY Brussels sprouts had been developed.

BRUSSELS SPROUTS

Flowering heads

In southern Europe, growers began selecting cabbages with large flowering heads. BY THE 15TH CENTURY, the flowering heads had become very large and the cauliflower had been developed. About a hundred years later broccoli was developed in Italy.

BROCCOLI

CAULIFLOWER

Tight clusters + flowering head = Cauliflower and broccoli

Tight clusters

A large cluster of tightly packed leaves called the cabbage "head" was developed by some people who began selecting seeds from kale plants with a tight cluster of leaves in the centre at the top of the stem. Over hundreds of successive generations, plants formed with tighter and larger cluster of leaves taking over the whole plant. This progress was completed in the 1ST CENTURY.

CABBAGE

Large leaves + tight clusters = Cabbage

Through a process of *artificial selection* the cabbage family is very WIDE and *varied*.

RED CABBAGE

PAK CHOI

By controlling the *pollination* process, growers can combine different cabbage plants and create new strange-looking varieties known as HYBRIDS. This process is called cross-pollination.

BROCCOFLOWER

WILD CABBAGE

In the beginning...

FAT STEM

Over the next 500 years, people were selecting kale plants with short fleshy stems. This selective process produced plants with fatter and fatter stems, which we call kohlrabi. Today, kohlrabi may have white, green, or purple stems.

KALE

Large leaves + fat stems = Kohlrabi

KOHLRABI

Large leaves

By the 5TH CENTURY BCE, a large crinkled-leaf plant had been developed, which we call kale. This is one of the oldest crops and is still grown today.

LEAFY VEGETABLE

The wild cabbage is a type of mustard plant that grows naturally around the Mediterranean Sea in Europe. ANCIENT PEOPLE collected its seeds and began growing it as a leafy vegetable. SEEDS FROM THE PLANTS WITH THE LARGEST LEAVES WERE SELECTED FOR THE NEXT YEAR'S CROP. Larger and larger-leafed plants were slowly being developed.

The struggle for existence

Many animals lay hundreds of eggs each year but few develop, hatch, and reach adulthood. Darwin recognized this, but it took him years to realize that this loss of life could be the driving force behind **evolution**.

Nine years before Darwin published *On the Origin of Species*, the poet Alfred Lord Tennyson wrote his poem *In Memoriam* (1850). It contained the phrase that came to represent people's hatred for Darwin's idea of natural selection in the 1800s:

"Nature, red in tooth and claw..."

In **1798**, the Reverend Thomas Malthus published *An Essay on the Principle of Population,* which argued that, in the case of humans, numbers are only controlled by famine and disease. His essay was to inspire Darwin's ideas about evolution.

I'M NOT AMUSED! IT'S 1838 – FORTY YEARS HAVE GONE BY AND DARWIN IS **ONLY JUST** GETTING AROUND TO READING MY ESSAY. TYPICAL!

"A plant which annually produces a thousand seeds, of which... only one comes to maturity, may be truly said to struggle."
Charles Darwin

If all the **froglets** survived, the world would be knee-deep in frogs *within 10 years.*

THE NUMBERS GAME

Out of **hundreds** of froglets:
- **Most** are eaten by predators;
- **Many** die from sickness;
- **Some** die from starvation;
- **Only** one or two live long enough to breed.

EEK! Not this way, chaps!

Frogs have hundreds of babies but only a few *survive!*

I *will* SURVIVE!

Darwin *recognized* that the individuals that SURVIVE and go on to reproduce tended to be the ones with a *competitive edge* over their rivals. These individuals were *"naturally selected"* to have offspring, which would be more likely to inherit the useful feature.

WINNING *characteristics* in nature:

Impressive feathers

The male peacock's tail seems clumsy, but to a female peacock looking for a mate, the males with the most "eyes" on their tails have an advantage. These individuals have been sexually selected. They would attract more females and have more offspring than plainer peacocks. Over time the feathers have become even more elaborate.

Tough antlers

Stags fight their rivals and the strongest ones with the largest antlers go on to mate and pass on their strength and the size of their antlers to their offspring. Over time the males have become much bigger than the females and have developed very large antlers as a result of sexual selection.

Well hidden

Red grouse are found in heather and black grouse are found in peaty areas. Their colourings keep them well camouflaged, protecting the grouse from predators. If black grouse had lived in heather, they would have been quickly spotted by predators and would not have survived to breed. The red grouse became more and more common in this environment.

Cross-fertilization

Flowering plants have *evolved to cross-fertilize* as these individuals can **OUT-COMPETE** the species that *self-fertilize*. Many of the bright flowers we see today have adapted to make sure they will be *cross-fertilized* to produce lots of healthy offspring.

BEST ADAPTED

For natural selection to work, there needs to be an existing feature that can be modified and improved upon. Darwin tested **insect-eating plants** called *sundews* to find out how they knew when to trap an insect but not be sensitive to a non-living object, such as a *feather*. Then he fed some with small pieces of MEAT and these grew *quicker* and produced **MORE** flowers than those that were not fed. He concluded that being able to trap and digest insects was a *favourable characteristic*.
Breakthrough!

I'm starving!

Explanation:

Insects carrying pollen from plant to plant had visited the uncovered plants and so these had been cross-fertilized to produce plants with good growth. The covered plants had not been visited by insects so had self-fertilized, producing plants with poor growth.

NOW TRY THIS!

TRY ONE OF DARWIN'S EXPERIMENTS: In the following test he showed that plant species had a selective advantage if they cross-pollinated with other individuals rather than self-pollinate. Darwin used common toadflax but any plant that produces seeds in a pod will do.

1. Grow six plants.
Cover three of the plants with fine netting to prevent insects getting to their flowers.

2. Wait
until the pods form. Select the five best pods from each of the covered and uncovered groups.

3. Count
the seeds in each pod and record the number for the covered and uncovered groups. What do you notice? You should find that the number of seeds is greater in the pods of the uncovered plants.

4. Now plant
ten seeds from the uncovered group and ten seeds from the covered group into pots. Label the groups. Keep all the seedlings warm and watered.

5. Measure
the height of the young plants. What do you notice? You should find that the plants whose seeds came from the covered group are shorter than the plants whose seeds came from the uncovered group.

Eye wonder

Darwin found the evolution of the human eye was one of the hardest cases to explain through natural selection. The structure and the way it works is so complex and seemingly so perfect. Despite knowing very little about the eye as compared to scientists' know-how today, Darwin stayed convinced that the human eye had adapted gradually from a simple to a complex organ. Each stage had been useful to the creature, and as the eye varied so the best variations were passed on.

HERE'S HOW SCIENTISTS TODAY THINK THE HUMAN EYE EVOLVED:

1

Light-sensitive spot

Nerve fibres

2

Pit

3

Retina

Transparent liquid

4

Cornea

Lens

Light-sensitive spot
Some creature in the past had a simple light-sensitive spot on its skin that gave it a slight competitive advantage, perhaps by being able to avoid a predator.

> I'm the sea-creature lancelet. My eye is just like your ancestor's.

Pinhole
Over time – calculated as 364,000 years by one scientist – a pit in the light-sensitive patch appeared in creatures, providing sharper vision. Maybe at about the same time, the front of the pit gradually narrowed, so light entered through a small hole, rather like the eye of a sea squirt.

Improved vision
During in-between stages, creatures' eyes developed with an increasing number of cells at the back, a greater curve of the surface, and a slight increase in transparency, rather like the eye of a hagfish.

> I'm a hagfish. I can see better in the ocean than that squirt!

Almost perfect
Eventually, the light-sensitive spot at the back became the retina with many cells receiving the image and a lens formed at the front of the eye, making the image clearer on the retina. A lamprey has very similar eyes to ours.

THE WATCHMAKER

In 1802, clergyman William Paley told a story about chancing upon a watch in a field. The watch had moving parts that worked together for a purpose. He concluded that as the existence of the watch proves that there was a watchmaker, so animals and plants prove the existence of a Creator. Followers of this "natural theology" argued: How could something so marvellous as the human eye have come about only by chance? The eye is complex like a pocket watch so it must have been designed perfectly adapted for its purpose by an intelligent designer.

Not quite the best ❺

A human has a single pair of moveable camera-type eyes. The lens can change shape to focus the image onto the back of the eye. But the design is not perfect as the optic nerve at the back of the eye has to pass through the light-sensitive retina that receives the image, causing a blind spot.

Lens

Cornea

This one
is yours!

Optic nerve

Iris

Retina

Transparent
liquid

TRY IT YOURSELF: Find your blind spot
Close you left eye and look at the +. Bring the image
closer and stop when you can no longer see the ●.

+   ●

Perfection

An octopus has a very similar camera-type eye to a human but it evolved separately and it does have many improvements. There is no blind spot because the nerves come from behind the retina. Another difference is that the lens is a fixed shape but moves closer to the retina to focus.

Retina

Cornea

Best
eye!

Optic
nerve

Lens

Iris

The whole
eyeball changes
shape to focus

Here's looking
at you, kid!

On the Origin of Species

In 1858, Darwin received a letter from young naturalist **Alfred Russel Wallace** that was to force him to publish his secret work of the past 20 years. A year later on 24th November, *1,250 copies* of a well-written and easy-to-read first edition of his theory of evolution by natural selection were printed, and said to have **sold out** on that first day.

A joint presentation

The man in Malaysia

One of Darwin's letter-writing friends was a young man called Alfred Russel Wallace who was travelling around the islands of Malaysia collecting specimens. In 1858, while recovering from a fever, Wallace had a flash of inspiration as he thought about the animals that lived and died on the islands. In that moment he had come to a similar conclusion as Darwin that the process of natural selection controlled the population size of living things.

Darwin was shocked by the content of Wallace's letter and was at a loss to know what to do. At this time, his ordered family life was in turmoil as two of his children were very ill. His beloved elder daughter Annie had died seven years earlier and he didn't want to lose another of his dear children. His daughter Henrietta recovered from her illness but unfortunately his youngest son died.

> I'll write *a letter to Charlie!* I wonder what he'll make of my idea?

> !*?

> By Jove! Alfie's *cracked* the theory, too.

> Darwin's friends, Lyell and Hooker, came to his aid and organized for a joint presentation of both his and Wallace's essays about evolution to be read to a group of scientists.

BESTSELLER

Bestseller

READ ALL ABOUT IT!

THE DAILY NEWS

104,000 COPIES SOLD

DARWIN CAUSES A STORM

In 1859, a very public and heated debate between critics and supporters of Charles Darwin's evolution theory erupted on the publication of his book *On the Origin of Species by means of Natural Selection*. But this uproar made everyone want to read it.

When the copyright of the first edition expired in 1901, the publishers had sold 56,000 copies of the original book and 48,000 copies of a cheap edition covered in paper or cheap cloth. After publication, Darwin said, "I had always feared and predicted an uproar, but I'm delighted about the success of my scientific book."

ON

THE ORIGIN OF SPECIES

BY MEANS OF NATURAL SELECTION,

OR THE

PRESERVATION OF FAVOURED RACES IN THE STRUGGLE
FOR LIFE.

By CHARLES DARWIN, M.A.,
FELLOW OF THE ROYAL, GEOLOGICAL, LINNÆAN, ETC., SOCIE
AUTHOR OF 'JOURNAL OF RESEARCHES DURING H. M. S. BEAGLE'S
ROUND THE WORLD.'

ON THE
ORIGIN
OF
SPECIES
DARWIN

Darwin outlined his theory of natural selection, justifying it with observations and evidence he had researched. The lengthy full title finally chosen was *On the Origin of Species by means of Natural Selection or the Preservations of Favoured Races in the Struggle for Life*. Editions have been printed all over the world.

Post-ORIGIN

Darwin continued to write a number of other books expanding on different aspects of his theory relating to plants and humans. But, in later life, he chose to specialize again in a detailed project – the actions of earthworms.

KEEP PLAYING! THEY'RE MOVING. HOW FASCINATING!

Worm charming

Darwin considered worms played a very important role in Earth's history and set out to prove this. One of his experiments involved his whole family playing different instruments to find out how the worms would respond. Darwin found that worms couldn't hear but would react to the vibrations if placed on an instrument.

MMMM, DINNER!

I'M FEELING VIBRATIONS.

IS IT A MOLE COMING? LET'S GET OUT OF HERE!

QUICK! IS IT RAINING? I LOVE THE WET.

NOW TRY THIS: Stick a garden fork into the soil and gently rock it to and fro. You'll notice earthworms coming to the surface.

TRUE or *false*

There have been a number of inaccurate statements made about Darwin's life and work. Below are a handful of some of these misconceptions to set the record straight:

Darwin came up with his **theory of evolution** while at the *Galápagos Islands.*

False. His ideas came later after his return from the voyage.

The *title* of Darwin's book is "Origin of the species".

False. By adding the "the" it implies that Darwin wrote about the origins of a particular species, which was not what the book is about.

Darwin came up with the phrase "survival of the fittest" to summarize his theory.

False. The philosopher Herbert Spencer coined this phrase.

A HERO'S BURIAL

When Darwin died in 1882, the scientific community wanted to honour him. Although Darwin had only requested a quiet funeral, his body was buried in a great ceremony at Westminster Abbey in London.

False. Darwin wrote only that monkeys, apes, and humans must have a common ancestor.

Darwin said, *"humans came from monkeys".*

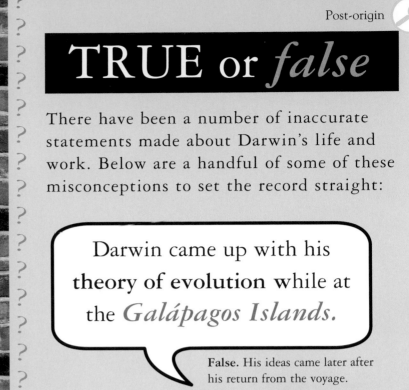

39

SQUEAK! YOU AND I HAVE THE SAME NUMBER OF GENES. LET'S BE FRIENDS!

ALL IN THE GENES

Today, we know something that Darwin had no idea about – genetics. By studying the microscopic chemical codes passed down from generation to generation, scientists have increased their understanding of how species have evolved.

We can now explain what makes us all unique and even trace ourselves back to common ancestors we share with other odd-looking creatures.

Not only does Darwin's natural selection theory hold up to this scientific scrutiny, but geneticists have also discovered other laws at work in nature. Their findings have also raised a number of ethical issues and aspects of evolution continue to cause very heated debates.

The pea plant puzzle

Hidden away in a monastery garden, a 19th-century Austrian monk, Gregor Mendel, was trying out experiments on pea plants. His tests were revealing that features were being passed down in many pieces of information from the parent plants to their offspring. We now call these pieces "genes".

Traits and characteristics

A trait is a feature and characteristics are the many forms of that feature. For example, the trait studied in this test is pod colour and the characteristics are either yellow or green.

These pieces represent the gene for the pea pod colour. P for green pods and p for yellow pods.

That's interesting! If the offspring get both a P and p piece then the plant shows the P feature. This copy must be stronger.

Gregor Mendel (1822–1884)

Test results

Mendel rubbed the pollen (male part) of one plant onto the stigma (female part) of the other plant.

The offspring have two copies of each gene – one from each parent.

How the two copies mix determines the pod colour.

CHROMOSOMES

Under the microscope, scientists looking into the cells of plants and animals discovered that the middle part, the nucleus, contained a number of thread-like shapes. These became known as chromosomes.

Different CHROMOSOMES contain different GENES.

Chromosome

Cell

Nucleus

Genes found along here.

Different LIVING THINGS have a different number of CHROMOSOMES.

The number does not have any connection with the complexity of the life form.

Mosquito
6 x

Puffer fish
42 x

Human
46 x

Servus! Ich heise Gregor.

If Mendel met Darwin

Although these two great chaps never met, if they did maybe their conversation would have gone like this:

Hello! My name is Charles.

MENDEL: Great idea about natural selection, Charles. God certainly moves in mysterious ways!

DARWIN: Thanks. It's surprising that no one had come up with the idea before. Mind you, I'm still not certain about how inheritance works.

MENDEL: Maybe I can help you with this. I've been doing some breeding experiments on pea plants. The results have been most interesting.

DARWIN: I found testing plants a useful way of finding out about something, too. Tell me about your tests.

MENDEL: Well, I placed the pollen from a pea plant with green pods on to the female part of a pea plant with yellow pods.

DARWIN: Did the offspring all have greenish-yellow pods?

MENDEL: No. All the offspring had green pods.

DARWIN: Oh! So the physical appearances were not a blend of the parents' characteristics.

MENDEL: That's right. I'm thinking that these "characters" were passed down from each parent unchanged. In each offspring, the characters from each parent separate and join with one set of the characters of the other parent. In this test, the stronger character – the green colour pod – appeared in all the offspring. That's not all!

DARWIN: What did you do next?

MENDEL: Well I took the pollen from one offspring and placed it on the female part of another offspring. And you'd never guess the result?

DARWIN: All the offspring had green pods again.

MENDEL: No! Most of these offspring did have green pods, but there were a few with yellow pods. Imagine my surprise.

DARWIN: Well, why do you think that happened?

MENDEL: I propose that tiny pieces of hereditary information are being passed down unchanged from generation to generation. This means that a weaker character – the yellow colour pod – that has been masked in one generation can reappear unchanged in another.

DARWIN: What else do you know about these pieces?

MENDEL: There's a piece for each of the traits determining seed shape, seed size, flower colour, pod shape, pod size, stem height, and so on. I've studied more than one trait at a time in the pea plants and noticed that, for example, the piece for pod colour is sorted separately from the piece for pod shape in each individual offspring.

DARWIN: Good work, Gregor. I wonder what these pieces look like and how they are linked together?

MENDEL: I'll have to leave that for future scientists to discover.

Dog
78 x

Goldfish
94 x

Human chromosomes are arranged in pairs, which are all matching except for the pair of sex chromosomes of a male. Chromosomes vary in size and shape depending on the number of genes they contain. Scientists arrange the pairs in order of size on a chart called a karyotype.

FEMALE HUMAN KARYOTYPE

Every body cell in a living thing contains the same number of chromosomes. Cells pass on their chromosomes when they divide to produce new cells. Every chromosome makes an exact copy of itself and then divides to make a new cell.

Genetic recipe

Instructions on how to build a living thing:

The packages: The hereditary material is divided into a number of packages called chromosomes found inside every cell.

CELL

CHROMOSOME

DNA

These chromosomes are made from strands of a chemical mix called deoxyribonucleic acid – or DNA for short.

GENE

Step-by-step instructions:
At specific places along the chromosomes are the genes. Each of these contains a sequence of DNA that provides the instructions, or code, to make the chemicals that form cells. When one or more genes are "switched on", each one (or each combination) reacts according to the instructions – how much, when, and where to make particular cells. In this way, the cell becomes a lung cell or a skin cell, and so on.

Mind-boggling and extremely complex investigations have been undertaken by scientists since the start of the 20th century to seek the complete picture of genetics (the study of heredity). But how does this help us to understand evolution?

THE GENOME

The big picture revealed so far is that all a living thing's inherited material is wrapped up in a genome. This is the *instruction manual* containing most of the basic information needed for building an individual.

The spiral ladder

The structure of DNA is shaped like a spiral ladder. The rungs make up a simple code represented by the four letters A, C, G, and T (shown as blue, red, yellow, and green), which stand for the base chemicals. Each rung has a pair of bases that splits in the middle when making an exact copy of itself for new cells.

EXTRACT YOUR DNA

ASK AN ADULT FOR PERMISSION AND HELP

YOU WILL NEED:

- a glass of salty water • a glass with 1 tsp washing-up liquid
- 3 tsp tap water • a clean teaspoon • 125 ml (4 fl oz) ice-cold alcohol (gin or vodka that's been in the freezer is ideal)

1. Swill the salty water around your mouth. *Do not swallow.*

2. Spit the contents of your mouth into the glass containing the washing-up liquid and tap water. Stir slowly with the clean teaspoon for a couple of minutes.

3. *Very slowly* pour the ice-cold alcohol down the inside of the glass so that it settles on top of the solution.
Leave for 2–3 minutes.

4. Observe the thin strands on top of the salty detergent mixture. This is your DNA.

If you wish, carefully remove the strand by twisting a plastic straw slowly in the glass. The strands will wrap around it, but they are very fragile. Once extracted you could stain the strands with food colouring to make them easier to see under a microscope.

THROW AWAY THE DNA AND THE LIQUID IN THE GLASS AFTER USE.

Mapping the genome

In 1990, an ambitious project involving many international scientists began to map out the complete sequence of the human genome. It took them 13 years to unravel the information for 3 billion rungs of the DNA ladder and identify the estimated 25,000 genes and where they were located. This team of scientists have also mapped the genomes of yeast, a roundworm, a mouse, and a fruit fly. Impressive! But, the findings raised more questions than answers.

There are a number of genes for which the uses are unknown. Some genes look a lot like genes found in very different living things, such as fish.

Why do the sizes of genomes vary so much between different species?

There's so much other stuff in DNA besides genes. What is it for and why do other living things have less of this "junk"?

DNA AND EVOLUTION

Thanks to understanding more about DNA, these strands of hereditary material provide the strongest proof for biological evolution – how genetic changes were made over time to make new species. By comparing the genomes of different living things and observing the changes in the coding of the genes, scientists can work out how closely different species relate to each other and even identify how long ago a common ancestor lived.

Our genomes are 96% **IDENTICAL** to a human's. Our differences are possibly due to where and when the genes have been switched on in the brain.

Humans have the same number of genes as mice. We carry the gene for making a tail but it gets switched off early in development. 90% of the genes linked to diseases are the same, which is why mice are so valuable for use in lab research on human illness.

550 million years ago humans had a common ancestor with the lancelet, a rod-like sea animal (see it on page 34).

We share about 31% of our genes with YEAST — a single living cell that replicates every 90 minutes.

All this thinking is making me hungry. Pass that banana!

We share 50% of our genes with a BANANA.

45

One in a quintillion

Your parents would have to have another 1,000,000,000,000,000,000 babies before one possibly might have the same genes as you. This genetic variation between individuals is the key to how species have evolved.

46 CHROMOSOMES IN PAIRS
This granddad has green eyes.

46 CHROMOSOMES IN PAIRS
This grandma has brown eyes.

46 CHROMOSOMES IN PAIRS
This granddad has blue eyes.

46 CHROMOSOMES IN PAIRS
This grandma has green eyes.

Each parent's 46 chromosomes are shuffled, divided, and half (23) are passed on to a child.

Studying twins

Identical twins have the same genes. By studying their traits, scientists have been able to work out which ones their genes have influenced and which their environment and upbringing have affected. Results have shown that genes affect appearance, eyesight, weight, IQ, and length of life, but have less influence on food preferences and sense of humour.

23 CHROMOSOMES
23 CHROMOSOMES

46 CHROMOSOMES IN PAIRS
This mum has brown eyes.

23 CHROMOSOMES

Answer: Half of your chromosomes that contain the genes have come from your mother and the other half from your father. Which half of their chromosomes you get and how these two sets of chromosomes come together is what makes you so unique, even from any brothers and sisters (unless you have an identical twin).

23 CHROMOSOMES

46 CHROMOSOMES IN PAIRS
This dad has green eyes.

23 CHROMOSOMES
23 CHROMOSOMES

Chip off the old block

Your appearance, your fingerprints, your voice, your health, and even how you clasp your hands have been coded by your genes. These genes have been passed down from your parents, who received their genes from their parents, who received their genes from their parents, and so on. You might have similar features to a family ancestor that have skipped a few generations. So how has this variation between us all happened?

Boy or girl?

Two of your chromosomes contain a gene that determines what sex you will be. These sex chromosomes are shaped like the letters X and Y. If you are a girl you have received an X-chromosome from both your parents, but if you are a boy you have one X-chromosome from your mother and one Y-chromosome from your father. For boys, all the genes on the X-chromosome are dominant as there is no matching pair, which means they might inherit genetic disorders from their mother. For example, colour blindness is a recessive gene that becomes dominant when passed on from mother to son.

Can you see a number in this circle of coloured dots? If not you might be colour blind. Test your family.

CHROMOSOMES 46 IN PAIRS

This child has blue eyes.

Human Genetics

HUMAN GENETICS like those of many other living things is not as simple as one gene for each trait. Often one gene can affect several traits or several genes can affect one trait, such as height or eye colour.

You get a set of genes affecting eye colour from both parents and if they are different then one set gets priority over the other – this is called the **DOMINANT**. Brown-eye genes are usually dominant over green-eye genes, which are dominant over blue-eye genes. The weaker of the set is called the **RECESSIVE**. To get the recessive feature, each parent must pass on a copy of the weaker genes. Often these features appear in grandparents and their grandchildren and skip their parents.

Diagram of the chromosome containing the genes that affect eye colour.

GREEN GENES

BROWN GENES

BLUE GENES

WHEN THE CHROMOSOMES COME TOGETHER TO FORM YOU, THERE ARE TWO SETS OF EVERY GENE.

Now TRY THIS! *Take the genes test to discover what you might have inherited.*

Can you roll your tongue into a U-shape?

Does the top bit of your little finger bend in towards the next finger?

Does your earlobe hang free at the bottom?

Do you have dimples in your cheeks when you smile?

Can you bend your thumb back more than 30°?

Does hair grow on the middle part of your toes?

Do you have freckles?

Does your nose tilt upwards?

Now test your family and relatives. Record their answers and trace the genes through your family tree.

Mutations

Every now and then, DNA within an individual's cells can become altered or damaged. These **random errors** are called **mutations**. When the changed DNA is passed on to their offspring, this causes genetic variation, which might be *naturally selected* for the **EVOLUTION** of a species.

WINNERS OR LOSERS?

Mutations are rare but over time they build up to have an effect. Inherited mutations can either have *no effect* on the individual, or have a *harmful* effect on the individual, or give the individual a *competitive advantage*. Through natural selection, the individual will either go on to breed and pass on its mutation or die and the mutation discontinues.

Neutral

Siamese cats have a mutated gene that causes kittens to be white at birth and then later to develop patches of colour at certain points on their faces, paws, and tails.

Helpful

Tigers have a mutated gene that gave them stripes. In the past, those with this gene were able to blend into the tall grasses and be more successful at catching food and surviving, so the mutated gene passed on to their offspring.

HOME, SWEET HOME

Whether a mutation is selected as harmful or helpful to individuals depends on their environment. In Antarctica, the sea is the best place to get food, so penguins have evolved through many small mutations to have webbed feet and stunted wings, perfect for swimming fast to catch food and escaping predators.

I've forgotten how to fly.

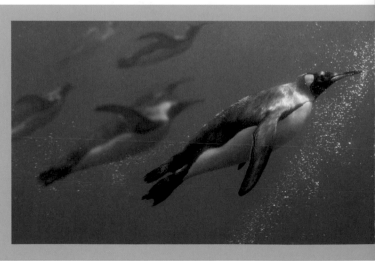

Inherited mutation *creates* **>** genetic variation *acted on by*

Who gets what?

Mutations can be inherited either from one parent or both parents depending on whether the change is on recessive (weak) or dominant (priority) genes. There's a 50% chance of inheriting a mutated dominant gene carried by one parent. However, there's only a 25% chance of inheriting a mutated recessive gene and even that depends on both parents being carriers.

My ancestors came from the Isle of Man.

Harmful

Manx cats carry a mutated gene that causes many kittens to be stillborn or die within their first year if inherited from both parents. If they only inherit the gene from one parent then the kittens do survive, but many have stumpy tails or no tails.

The Manx gene is dominant. Cats that carry the gene (M) pass it on to half their offspring.

However, these mutations are useless on land. Penguins would be unable to survive in an environment without water.

WHAT CAN GO WRONG?

DNA can get altered

when cells are dividing and the copying process of the chromosomes goes wrong. A gene could be copied wrongly. If a chromosome breaks or an extra gap appears in the DNA sequence, a gene is unlikely to work. When an extra chromosome number 21 appears in a cell, this mutation causes physical and mental differences known as Down's syndrome.

21

DNA can be broken

when radiation or chemicals affect the body and the cells are unable to repair themselves completely. If this damage affects the reproductive cells then the mutation could be inherited. As humans spread around the world, the amount and quality of sunlight (ultraviolet radiation) absorbed by the cells altered the DNA of the skin colour gene.

UV radiation causes a bulge in the DNA sequence

Sections of DNA can move

to another position on the chromosomes, often causing gene mutations. The colour patterns in maize are due to these "jumping" genes.

Moveable sections of DNA either copy themselves so there are duplicate copies on the chromosomes or are "cut and pasted" from one chromosome to another as shown here.

Original chromosomes

Changed chromosomes

4   20   4   20

> natural selection = evolution of species

WE'RE ALL

All living things are mutants, including us, as we have all evolved from mutated genes, setting us apart from each other. Some mutated genes cause rare conditions and these get carried along, hidden within the DNA sequence of "carrier" individuals. Every now and then, when a carrier or carriers have offspring, the condition reappears.

Ghostly

The genes affecting skin, hair, or feather colour have been mutated to reduce the amount of pigment (colour) in a condition called leucism. The animal appears white, which means it can be spotted easily by prey and predators.

Hairless

Some people have a human hairless gene, which means they lose all their hair very quickly after birth. They not only have no hair on their head, but also have no eyebrows, no eyelashes, no nasal hair, and no body hair. They need extra protection from the sun and bacteria.

Better than one?

In the early stages as a developing embryo (egg), this snake started out as twins, but then due to a gene defect stopped, leaving two heads on one body. Often the two heads disagree and might even try to swallow each other.

MUTANTS

Extra digits

A gene for six digits causes the cells making the fingers or toes during early development to keep working. It's a dominant gene so it takes priority but it's also extremely rare.

I'm Stumpy.
I'm famous for being born with two extra legs in February, 2007.

Now try this!

Draw a picture or use a photograph of yourself. Change three of your features by changing the size or the colour, adding more, or removing.

Can you think of any situations in which these mutations might be naturally selected to give you a competitive advantage?

For example, make your thumbs larger to help you move the games console controls faster. This inherited mutation might be naturally selected as a useful adaptation in a technology-driven environment.

NOT IMPOSSIBLE! A PANDA'S THUMB IS AN ENLARGED WRIST BONE — A MUTATION THAT WAS NATURALLY SELECTED AS IT GIVES THE ANIMAL AN EXCELLENT GRIP ON ITS FAVOURITE FOOD, BAMBOO.

Twists of fortune...

Ready for another evolutionary bombshell that Darwin didn't consider? Natural selection is not the only process affecting *which genes make it* through to the next generation. Completely at RANDOM,

KEY

= This shape represents the changing size of the gene pool of the red kite species.

3 The gene pool also INCREASES when new genes are introduced. This happens when different populations breed with each other. This transfer of genes is called *gene flow*.

2 The gene pool INCREASES when a mutated gene survives. Natural selection is at work, selecting the variations that are best adapted to the environment.

1 The total of all the genes of a species is called the gene pool. This includes all the many variations of all the genes.

European populations of red kites followed migration patterns south across Europe to North Africa and back. Individuals from the different populations would breed with each other.

Red kites are predators and scavengers, and evolved impressive wingspans and excellent eyesight, enabling them to seek out animal carcasses on the ground.

4 The gene pool DECREASES when animals die or don't breed. The random process of genetic drift might be more noticeable in a small population, reducing the number of genetic variations.

This is the story of the red kite species, so far. Populations of the red kite ranged across North and Central Europe and North Africa.

START

Since the 1500s, the red kites in Britain were considered pests and were being killed. As the kite became rare, many were caught and stuffed for collections. By the late 1800s, populations of red kites in England and Scotland were extinct and only a handful of pairs were left in remote parts of Wales.

NATURAL SELECTION + GENETIC DRIFT

or fate

some genetic variations make it through while others don't and are lost forever. This process is called **genetic drift** and is more noticeable when it occurs in small populations.

8 **The process of natural selection** continues, selecting the most advantageous genetic variations.

THE FUTURE

The populations in the wild have increased in number and continue to breed successfully. The trait to migrate has been inherited, which means there is a future possibility of further gene flow.

7 **Conserving a species** does not just increase the population size but also creates a gene pool with many variations by introducing individuals from other populations, giving more chance of survival.

Sometimes a kite from the Welsh population is born with white feathers. Rare, often harmful, mutations become more evident in populations that have been through a genetic bottleneck.

During the 1990s, red kites from Sweden, Spain, Germany, and Wales were released into suitable habitats in Scotland and England.

5 **When species drop** to very low numbers and then increases again, they are said to pass through a *genetic bottleneck*.

9 **Random events** may wipe out individuals with selectively-advantageous genes. The lottery of which genes make it through continues.

6 **Species close to extinction** face a number of problems due to having a small gene pool.

In the 1930s, the number of red kites was so low that only one female bird remained. The population slowly increased but all were her descendants.

The habitat of the Welsh red kites had a harsh climate and a limited food supply. The population recovered slowly during the mid-1900s because of pesticides and a disease that killed their rabbit prey.

Kites are being killed or injured by the blades of wind turbines, and poisoned by the illegal poison baits left out for foxes and crows, and by eating poisoned rats. One kite has been killed by colliding with a jet fighter aircraft.

= SIZE OF GENE POOL

Mystery of *mysteries*

SOUTH
AMERICA

How do new species form? Darwin referred to this question as "the mystery of mysteries". There are many explanations of how this process called speciation works, but most scientists agree that on islands, geographical isolation is a major factor. The many species of finches of the Galápagos Islands are famous for being studied by Darwin, but they continue to be an excellent example of how new species evolve.

EQUATOR

Pacific
Ocean

THE
GALÁPAGOS
ISLANDS

Adaptation

Over the last three million years, the Galápagos islands have changed. New islands have appeared, the climate has become more varied, and so the food sources – plants and animals – have changed, too. Although weak fliers, the finches have been blown to other islands and adapted to fill a niche in their new situations.

SEPARATION

Around three million years ago, a group of ground finches from South America were blown across to an island in the Galápagos. Separated from their own population, these seed-eating birds arrived in a cloud-forest habitat that was full of different things to eat. Their descendants gradually adapted to occupy their own niche. Their body size changed as some moved from the ground to the trees and their beak shape changed as some fed on fruit, nectar, insects, or spiders.

Speciation is like some characters in a story going off on an adventure that changes their looks

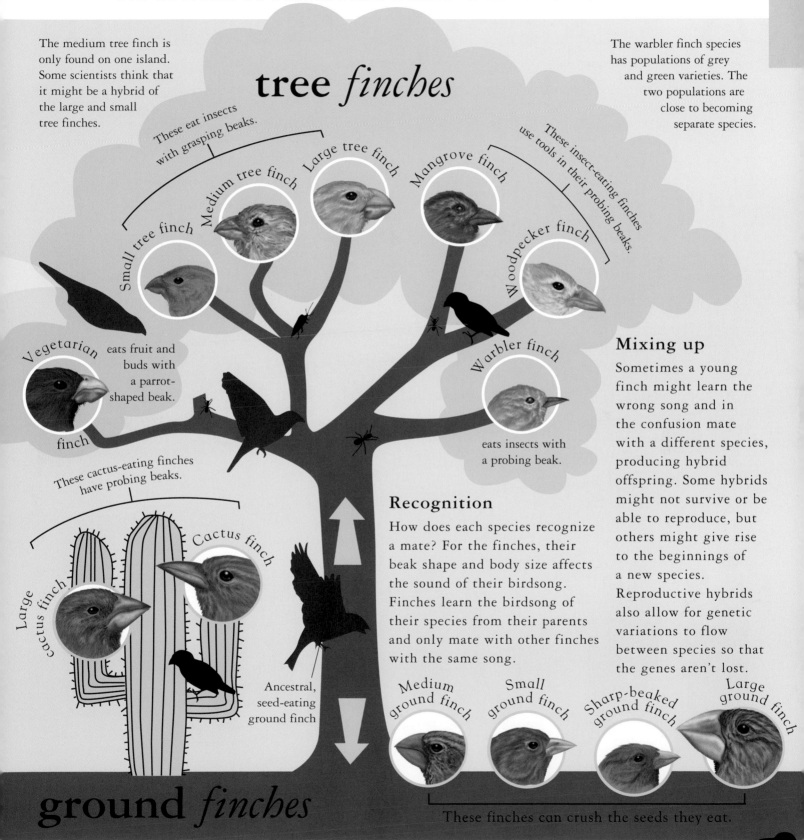

A **new species** *is achieved when* **two populations**
of the same living thing become so **different** *that they can*
NO LONGER SUCCESSFULLY BREED WITH EACH OTHER.

The medium tree finch is only found on one island. Some scientists think that it might be a hybrid of the large and small tree finches.

The warbler finch species has populations of grey and green varieties. The two populations are close to becoming separate species.

tree *finches*

These eat insects with grasping beaks.

Small tree finch

Medium tree finch

Large tree finch

Mangrove finch

These insect-eating finches use tools in their probing beaks.

Woodpecker finch

Vegetarian eats fruit and buds with a parrot-shaped beak. **finch**

Warbler finch

eats insects with a probing beak.

Mixing up

Sometimes a young finch might learn the wrong song and in the confusion mate with a different species, producing hybrid offspring. Some hybrids might not survive or be able to reproduce, but others might give rise to the beginnings of a new species. Reproductive hybrids also allow for genetic variations to flow between species so that the genes aren't lost.

These cactus-eating finches have probing beaks.

Cactus finch

Large cactus finch

Recognition

How does each species recognize a mate? For the finches, their beak shape and body size affects the sound of their birdsong. Finches learn the birdsong of their species from their parents and only mate with other finches with the same song.

Ancestral, seed-eating ground finch

Medium ground finch

Small ground finch

Sharp-beaked ground finch

Large ground finch

ground *finches*

These finches can crush the seeds they eat.

and behaviour so much that when they return home,
they are no longer recognized.

A GHOST in

Genes remember the past.

This is the theory some scientists have recently suggested. The lives of your grandparents when they were growing up – the air they breathed, the food they ate, how they felt, and the things they saw – affect your health and behaviour, and how you live your life will affect your grandchildren. It's not just DNA we're inheriting but these influences tagging along on top of it.

ENVIRONMENT

- Car exhausts
- Cigarette smoke
- Pollution
- Mobile phone waves

YOU ARE...

what your grandparents breathed in. A grandparent's exposure to an industrial poison may be the cause of a certain cancer in their grandchildren.

What we do to our bodies...

could affect **our** grandchildren – how happy they will be, how much they eat, and what diseases they may get.

your *genes*

EMOTION

♥ • *Love*
  • HATE
♥ • *Stress*
  • CALM
  • Hardship

FOOD AND DRINK

🍴 • Sweets
   • Pesticides on food
   • Alcohol
🥤 • Canned drinks
   • Additives

CHEMICALS

💊 • Spray-on creams
   • Injections
   • Drugs, including
     medicines

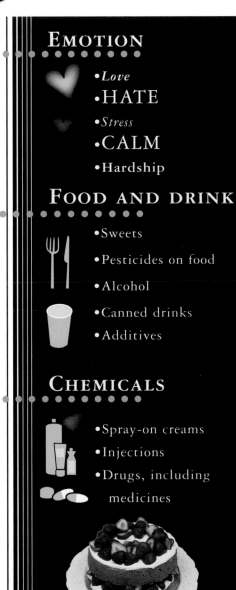

YOU ARE...

what your grandparents ate.
The amount of food our
grandparents ate affects
whether our genes will be able
to cope with how much or how
little we eat. If they ate well,
then we are more likely to live
longer if we eat well than
if we eat less.

THE SWITCHBOARD

Every cell carries the entire genetic
code in its DNA. Switching genes
on and off affects what that cell
will be used for – a lung cell, a
skin cell, a brain cell, an eye cell,
and so on.

What's controlling the switches?

DNA contains the instruction code
for controlling genes, but it can
be affected by chemical tags that
override the DNA instructions.
These tags add up over a lifetime
and are caused by lifestyle habits.
Tags not only cause immediate
changes but may also be inherited
by the next generation.

These tags cause changes by
hiding certain genes, switching
them off, which makes
another gene switch
on instead. Faulty
switches cause health
and behaviour
problems, such as
obesity (overweight),
diabetes (too much
sugar in blood),
mental illness,
cancers (when the
cells divide too
quickly), and
heart disease.

chemical tag

A tag hides the gene, switching it off.

Another gene gets switched on.

Scientists are
studying whether
they can control
these switches. If so,
maybe one day they
can switch diseased cells
back to being normal.

Does this theory sound familiar?

Remember Chevalier
de Lamarck from page 13 and his
idea that animals were changed
within their lifetime by their
environment? He had a good idea
but used the wrong examples!

For the *good* of the SPECIES?

Honeybees, army ants, and social wasps belong to a group of insects that form large and highly organized colonies. Evolution is driven by individuals successfully passing on their genes to the next generation. However, these colonies have only a few individuals that have offspring and the rest just work to look after the offspring. So why have colonies evolved?

Each individual has a job to do within the colony.

A queen mates with many males over several days to get a good mix of genes. Then over many years she lays a mix of fertilized and unfertilized eggs.

The fertilized eggs become the female bees, of which most will be the workers, and the non-fertilized eggs become the male bees called drones.

Workers perform *a waggle dance* to direct other workers to where they have found food. A gene is thought to control the change in behaviour during the life of the worker.

MALE DRONE

Young workers feed the larvae and tend the nest. They control how many female larvae are fed royal jelly to become queen bees and how many male larvae survive.

After three weeks, the workers leave the nest to gather food. Older workers collect pollen and nectar.

But are the workers doing their job for the good of

FAMILY FORTUNES

WHY might a bird stay in a nest to help care for their parents' next brood as the young male white-fronted African bee eater does?

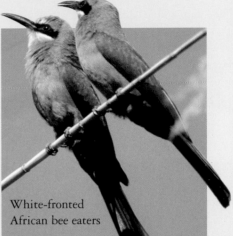

White-fronted African bee eaters

This type of self-sacrificing behaviour occurs in a number of groups of animals. The behaviour improves survival rates of relatives' offspring. But is this for the good of the family or is there a hidden motive? An individual shares 50% of its genes with each parent and with its brothers and sisters, and has 25% in common with nieces and nephews. By helping the group, the individual is ensuring that many of its genes survive. It also might learn some good parenting skills before having a family of its own.

SUPER-SISTERS

Why don't worker honeybees have offspring? Unusually, male bees come from unfertilized eggs so have only half (16) the number of chromosomes as a female bee. A male passes on an exact copy of his chromosomes to his daughters, while the female queen only passes on half of hers.

Queen 32 × Male 16

16 16 eggs + 16 sperm

Male unfertilized 16   Females fertilized 32 32

This means that the workers that have the same father are super-sisters, sharing 75% of their genes (which is more than if they had their own offspring). So, by raising their larval super-sisters to reach adulthood, the workers are ensuring that more of their genes are carried in the hive.

the colony or for their own benefit?

Playing God

We can now do a great deal to *alter* not only our OWN GENES but those of every other animal and plant. But our ability to *manipulate* genes can have positive and *negative* effects. Just because we can do something, DOESN'T ALWAYS MEAN WE SHOULD. As in all debates, there are *pros* and *cons* to be considered.

Biodiversity

The number of species on this planet and the way they interact are important in maintaining the health and survival of all organisms. However, human activity is driving many species to extinction. This loss of species could have disastrous consequences. When a colony dies, its genes go with it. If the gene pool shrinks, variation decreases and can limit the ability of an organism to adapt to change. This leaves any remaining members of the species vulnerable to a sudden change in their environment. If this species is a key link in a food chain, it may also affect organisms that depend on it.

EXTINCT

EXTINCT

EXTINCT

Reduced biodiversity MAY result in

FOOD CROPS

A large root system helps plants to absorb more water and nutrients. The plant on the right has been genetically modified to grow bigger and better roots.

Scientists are trying to develop *crops* with improved characteristics using biotechnology. *Their main aims* are to help crops grow in *difficult environments*, improve their nutritional value, and make them more resistant to pests. *Opponents* of these crops argue that bioengineered genes *might escape* into the environment and could affect *wild* varieties, and may also have unknown consequences on *humans* and animals eating them.

DESIGNER BABIES

Advances in science mean that not only can people who were unable to have children now have them, but in some cases they can choose for their baby to have certain traits. This is useful if there is a genetic disease in the family that is only carried by or affects one sex. But while many people think this is an acceptable use of gene technology, scientists are coming under pressure to select for other traits, such as hair or eye colour. The ethics of whether this is a desirable thing to do are only just starting to be debated.

CLONING

Cloning is the technique of taking a cell from an animal or plant, extracting its DNA, and inserting it into another cell to create an exact copy of the original organism. Those in favour of cloning point to its benefits in spreading superior genes over larger populations of animals and plants rather than waiting for the results of crossbreeding. Those against point to the unknown effects of these genes on the health and biodiversity of species.

the loss of potentially useful genes.

Jurassic Park

Could we bring back the dinosaurs? They did it in the movies, but is it technically possible? And do we *really* want to?

Back to the bird

Re-creating an extinct animal is much harder in real life than it is in the movies. Scientists face a number of *problems*, the main one being that DNA, an animal's genetic code, does not survive for long once the animal is dead. **Most fossils**, including those of the dinosaurs, *are too old to recover any DNA*. One way around the problem would be to start with an existing animal and work backwards. We know that birds are descended from the dinosaurs, so it may be possible to RE-CREATE A DINO by switching genes on or off in birds. Scientists have already managed to make bird embryos grow longer tails and feathers on their scaly legs.

But what would we do with a DINOSAUR even if we did manage to grow a new one?

GRRR!!

THE BIGGEST BIRD EGG YOU COULD USE TO MAKE A DINOSAUR IS THAT OF AN OSTRICH. THIS COULD GROW A DINO THE SIZE OF A VELOCIRAPTOR.

Tyrannosaurus rex was one of the most fearsome predators that ever lived.

Rare as hen's teeth

Birds have not had teeth for 70 million years, but researchers have found them in the embryos of mutant chickens. It is thought birds lost their teeth to grow beaks instead, but still have the potential to make them. The teeth were just like those of a crocodile — another relative of the dinosaur.

Teeth forming in the beak of a chicken

In the film *Jurassic Park*, scientists extracted dinosaur DNA from **BLOOD** in the gut of an insect **trapped in amber**. Scientists have attempted to do this in *real life*, but with little success. Instead, they found that these insects **CARRIED DISEASES** that could have helped to **kill-off** the dinosaurs.

Making the switch

Scientists have taken DNA from an extinct Tasmanian tiger and planted it into a mouse embryo to see what would happen. They found that the DNA switches on a gene that makes cartilage that later becomes the mouse's limb and tail bones. Even though it won't bring back the Tasmanian tiger, this shows that extinct genes can be made to work again.

Cartilage forming in limbs and tail

So *that's* what it does!

Mammoth task

We probably have more chance of re-creating mammoths than bringing back dinosaurs. They only became extinct around 10,000 years ago and some have been found frozen in ice. Ice preserves DNA, so it might be possible to take the eggs or sperm from frozen mammoths and implant them in an Asian elephant. This could give us an animal that is at least 50% mammoth.

I may not look scary but I have great potential!

Moorhen's wing claw

From wings to forelimbs

You can't usually see the fingers in a bird's wing, but they sometimes appear as claws in baby birds, such as moorhens or hoatzins. Since the genes are already there, it may be possible to transform a bird's wings back into the front claws of a dinosaur.

Archaeopteryx, one of the first birds, had teeth, claws on its wings, and a long tail.

EVOLUTION IN ACTION

Many of Darwin's theories about evolution were based on his careful observations of how things looked and worked. However, many vital bits of information were missing, and he could only hope that new discoveries would prove him right.

Today, scientists are beginning to fill in many of the gaps. New fossils have been found, and DNA technology is uncovering surprising connections between plant and animal species. Even so, there is still a long way to go in our understanding of evolution.

There remains one **BIG** question: *Are humans still evolving, or have we reached our limits?* We can only wait and see.

Story of life

Our planet is 4,500 million years old. In its early days, Earth was a hot rock surrounded by poisonous gases. A cocktail of chemicals was washed into the oceans, where they reacted and formed molecules that began to copy themselves. Small changes in these molecules allowed better copiers, called nucleic acids, to dominate. This was the start of natural selection.

Underwater events

Some scientists think life may have begun around vents on the seabed. These vents blast out hot chemicals from the centre of the Earth, and could have provided the energy for them to combine into bigger molecules.

The ability of molecules (groups of atoms) to join and copy themselves was a key step in the development of life.

Cyanobacteria

Living stromatolites in Australia

3,800 MYA SIMPLE SINGLE-CELL BACTERIA APPEAR

CYANOBACTERIA OXYGENATE EARTH'S POISONOUS OCEANS

3,200 MYA ATMOSPHERIC OXYGEN INCREASES

4,000

3,600 million years ago (mya)

3,200 mya

Cells

Once an efficient copying mechanism had developed into the complex chemical DNA, the next step was to enclose it in a membrane that would protect it from the external environment. These simple organisms were prototypes of the first bacteria.

Stepping up the gas

The appearance of cyanobacteria (blue-green algae) was the first step towards making Earth's oceans inhabitable. These produced oxygen using photosynthesis, a process that uses sunlight to turn carbon dioxide and water into sugars and oxygen.

Stromatolites

Stromatolites are rock structures formed by mats of cyanobacteria. They released oxygen into the atmosphere, where it reacted with ultraviolet light to form a protective layer of ozone around Earth that shields life from harmful rays.

First animals

The first major evidence of multicellular animals is seen in the Ediacaran fossils of Canada. These are mainly soft-bodied, worm- or jelly-like animals, but they show that many new body shapes had already evolved.

Lichens are a combination of an alga and a fungus that live together.

Protists are single or multicelled organisms that have a nucleus. They are the ancestors of all plants, fungi, and animals.

This fossil from the Precambrian period is thought to be an Ediacaran jellyfish.

I'M HALLUCIGENIA AND I'VE GOT LEGS, SPINES, AND A LONG GUT. IT'S A SPECIES-EAT-SPECIES WORLD OUT THERE!

Lichens

Lichens were the first complex organisms to colonize the land. They absorbed large amounts of carbon dioxide from the atmosphere and replaced it with oxygen. As the carbon dioxide levels went down, the temperature cooled, which may have triggered a series of global ice ages. The increase in oxygen also allowed early animals to grow bigger and more complicated.

BOOM CAMBRIAN EXPLOSION

The sudden appearance of lots of new fossil species at the beginning of the Cambrian period puzzled Darwin. This explosion of life forms may have occurred after a rapid rise in oxygen levels or because a large number of new habitats became available.

1,800 MYA
FIRST COMPLEX LIFE FORMS (PROTISTS)

635 MYA
END OF LAST SNOWBALL EARTH

700 mya   •   630 mya   542

1,300 MYA
FIRST FUNGI

Snowball Earth

Earth turned into a giant snowball several times in its early history. Despite ice hundreds of metres thick, some algae, bacteria, and fungi managed to survive because they contained proteins that had evolved to work in the cold.

Snack attack

Many of the creatures that evolved in the early Cambrian have features that show animals had begun to eat each other. A single gummy bite may have been behind the evolution of teeth, feet, guts, spines, and hard shells.

Cambrian
period 542–488 mya

The Cambrian was when animal life forms really began to diversify. What little land there was above sea level lay clustered around the equator. Because the atmosphere still had little oxygen everything lived in the sea. Sponges, worms, molluscs, and reef-building animals were abundant. Trilobites, a group of hard-shelled invertebrates, made their first appearance. Many of the Cambrian animals had weird shapes and features that are no longer seen. Land plants had not yet evolved.

TRILOBITES DOMINATED THE SEAS FOR 300 MILLION YEARS. THEY HAD UNIQUE EYES THAT ENABLED THEM TO SEE THEIR PREY.

Ordovician
period 488–443 mya

The continents had begun to move together by the beginning of the Ordovician and would end up covered in ice at the South Pole. The first corals appeared, along with snails, clams, and squid-like animals. Armoured jawless fish swam among sea lilies growing up from the seafloor. A few arthropods began to take their first tentative steps on to the land.

SEA LILIES WERE ACTUALLY ANIMALS, RELATED TO MODERN STARFISH AND FEATHER STARS.

Silurian
period 443–416 mya

The melting of the ice that had formed at the end of the Ordovician caused a huge rise in sea level. Many species had died out, creating opportunities for others to take over. The numbers of jawless fish increased and they began to colonize freshwater rivers. At the same time fish with jaws appeared. Giant scorpions roamed the seabed and corals formed large reefs. The first plants began to colonize the land.

THE FIRST LAND PLANTS LOOKED VERY LIKE MODERN WHISK FERNS, WHICH HAVE SIMPLE ROOTS.

542mya

488mya

443mya

Cothurnocystis elizae

Brand **NEW** *shell* suit

BRACHIOPODS (LAMPSHELLS) WERE COMMON ON THE CAMBRIAN SEAFLOOR. THEY STILL EXIST TODAY, BUT THERE ARE FEWER SPECIES.

THIS **STRANGE** CREATURE IS THOUGHT TO BE THE **ANCESTOR** OF **ALL** ANIMALS WITH A BACKBONE, INCLUDING HUMANS.

THE FIRST FISH HAD **NO JAWS**. IN SOME, THE HEAD WAS COVERED BY A **BONY PLATE** THAT ACTED LIKE A **SHIELD**. THEY ALSO HAD AN INTERNAL SKELETON TO SUPPORT THE MUSCLES.

Devonian Carboniferous Permian
period 416–359 mya   period 359–299 mya   period 299–251 mya

Life in the water was dominated by fish – primitive sharks began to increase in number and the first bony and lobe-finned fish appeared. Ammonites were the latest molluscs to arrive and trilobites began to decline. By the end of the period the lobe-finned fish had begun to walk on their fins and haul themselves on to the land as the first tetrapods. Plants were diverging rapidly on land, providing homes for wingless insects.

Large primitive trees now dominated coastal swamps and formed huge forests. Tetrapods started to walk on land and evolve into amphibians. Insects grew wings and took to the air. Marine life flourished – molluscs, corals, and crinoids were abundant. Sharks were also common and diverse. At the end of the period the first reptiles emerged from eggs that could be laid on land.

All the continents joined together to form the supercontinent Pangaea. This reduced the length of coastline and many marine animals became extinct. The interior became a massive desert. The first seed plants (conifers) and mosses appeared. Amphibians and reptiles began to diversify, including groups that would go on to become dinosaurs and mammals.

A fossil tree trunk

One *small* step for a **TETRAPOD**, one giant leap for evolution.

EVER WONDERED WHERE **COAL** COMES FROM? SWAMPS WERE IDEAL FOR PRESERVING THE TRUNKS OF MILLIONS OF TREES. DEAD TRUNKS WERE COVERED IN MUD AND PRESSED TO FORM COAL SEAMS.

DIMETRODON WAS A MAMMAL-LIKE REPTILE WITH SPECIAL TEETH FOR EATING MEAT.

416mya   359mya   299mya

A breath of fresh air...

Now try this!
Find out about the rocks in your area and the geological time periods they belong to (the local library or museum should be able to help). Then collect pictures of fossils that have been found in these rocks and make a map of what was living in your neighbourhood millions of years ago.

LUNGFISH WERE A TYPE OF LOBE-FINNED FISH THAT EVOLVED A **LUNG** AS WELL AS GILLS TO HELP THEM GULP AIR FROM THE SURFACE.

COELACANTHS WERE A GROUP OF FISH THAT WERE THOUGHT TO HAVE GONE EXTINCT AT THE END OF THE CRETACEOUS, UNTIL ONE WAS CAUGHT IN 1938.

Triassic
period 251–199 mya

Jurassic
period 199–145 mya

Cretaceous
period 145–65 mya

The warm and dry conditions of the Triassic were ideal for reptiles to flourish on land. They also flew in the sky (pterosaurs) and swam in the sea (ichthyosaurs). Early crocodiles and turtles inhabited riverbanks. In the sea, ammonites were abundant and the first starfish and sea urchins appeared. Conifers, gingkos, cycads, and seed ferns took over from coal-forming trees, and the first flowering plants sprouted. Small nocturnal mammals survived the extinction that marked the end of the period.

The Jurassic is famous as the age of the dinosaurs. Huge sauropods ate cycads and ferns and were preyed on by meat-eating allosaurs and megalosaurs. The first birds evolved from small, feathery dinosaurs. Modern sharks appeared and amphibians began to look more like modern frogs and toads. Pangaea began to split apart, flooding large areas of land.

The modern continents began to take shape. This was the time of the giant dinosaurs, particularly meat eaters such as *Tyrannosaurus rex*. Flowering plants started to spread and insects diversified to pollinate them. Birds pushed the pterosaurs to extinction. New mammals emerged, including the ancestors of the marsupials.

EARLY **BIRDS** STILL LOOKED LIKE THEIR **DINOSAUR** ANCESTORS, WITH **TEETH** AND **WING CLAWS**.

RUN
boys!

MODERN MAGNOLIAS (RIGHT) HAVE CHANGED VERY LITTLE SINCE THEY FIRST EVOLVED (LEFT).

251 mya

199 mya

145 mya

THE **ICHTHYOSAUR**, A DOLPHIN-LIKE REPTILE, SWAM IN **TRIASSIC** SEAS.

SAUROPODS SUCH AS THE **BRACHIOSAURUS** WERE LARGE, PLANT-EATING DINOSAURS.

Megazostrodon
Megazostrodon was a tiny shrew-like mammal. Its hair kept it warm while it searched for food at night. It laid eggs and looked after its young.

Tertiary
period 65–1.8 mya

Quaternary
period 1.8 mya to present

Mass extinction

The end of the Cretaceous is marked by the extinction of a large number of species, including the dinosaurs. No one is sure what happened, but many think Earth was hit by an asteroid. This threw up clouds of dust that changed the climate and disrupted food chains. The survivors were those that could adapt to new conditions.

Mammals took over the role of the largest life forms and diversified to fill habitats left by reptiles and dinosaurs. Most of the modern forms of fish, invertebrates, birds, insects, and flowering plants evolved during this period. The first hominins (early forms of humans) appeared at the end of the period. The climate began to cool dramatically, favouring the rise of grasslands and grazing animals.

AT 6 M (20 FT) TALL, **GIANT SLOTHS** WERE TOO BIG TO HANG AROUND IN TREES.

TYRANNOSAURUS REX

This period started with an ice age. The continents had reached their current positions but a number of land bridges allowed species to cross continents. Giant mammals, such as mammoths, had adapted to the cold but began to die out as the climate warmed. Hunting by humans may have speeded up the process. Large carnivores, such as sabre-toothed cats and cave bears, also vanished. Many species of humans evolved and died out, leaving *Homo sapiens* as the sole survivor.

SABRE-TOOTHED CATS WERE THE MOST **FEROCIOUS** PREDATORS OF THEIR DAY.

65mya

1.8mya

OUR EARLIEST **ANCESTORS** APPEARED ABOUT 5 MILLION YEARS AGO.

And here we are

Modern man, *Homo sapiens*, emerged 250,000 years ago. Until 25,000 years ago we lived alongside the Neanderthals, who were stronger and more stockily built. It is not clear what happened to them.

71

Missing links

One of the biggest problems Darwin faced in his theory of evolution were gaps in the fossil record that showed evolutionary changes. Geology was a new science at the time and dating rocks and fossils was difficult. Since then, many new discoveries have been made that are helping to fill in the gaps.

From scales to feathers

One of the first "missing links" to be found was *Archaeopteryx*, a winged fossil that showed a change, or transition, from a dinosaur to a bird. A number of other fossils have since been found, including a non-flying dromaeosaur that had downy feathers from head to tail, suggesting feathers may first have evolved as a way to keep warm.

Fishapods

Tiktaalik, a transitional form between a fish and a walking tetrapod, shows how this "fishapod" had developed wrist and finger bones that enabled it to prop itself up on its fins. Holes on top of its head suggest it may have breathed air through primitive lungs.

Written in stone

This page from an 1880 book shows how naturalists and geologists attempted to match the fossils they had found to the sequence of rocks in their area.

Frogs and salamanders

An ancestor of frogs and salamanders that shows features of both was identified in 2008. *Gerobatrachus hottoni* is like a salamander in shape but has a frog-like head and jaw. Frogs and salamanders are now thought to have split into separate species between 240 and 275 million years ago.

MISSING LINK

The "Abominable Mystery"

Darwin's "abominable mystery" was how flowering plants had managed to spread and diversify in a short space of time. In 2006 researchers discovered a shrub on a Pacific island that could have been one of the first flowering plants to evolve 130 million years ago. The Amborella bush has a unique way of making seeds, which may show it had a conifer ancestor. There are now more than 400,000 species of flowering plants on Earth.

Platypus

When the first example of a platypus was sent from Australia everyone thought it had been faked using bits from a bird, a reptile, and a mammal. Genetic testing has now shown that it really is a mixture of all three. The platypus is the earliest mammal offshoot from the reptiles. It lays eggs but produces milk like other mammals. It also seems to have evolved the ability to produce venom independently of its reptile ancestors.

Evolution of mammalian ear

The evolution of the mammalian ear can be clearly tracked through fish, amphibian, and reptile fossils. Mammals have three tiny bones in the inner ear that began as the jaw bones of fish. Over time they changed form and function, shrank, and moved away from the jaw. This allowed mammals to develop a superior sense of hearing.

MISSING LINK

MAMMAL

REPTILE

AMPHIBIAN

FISH

NOW TRY THIS!

Pick any two animals that look very different, such as a fish and a crocodile, a lizard and a bird, or a reptile and a mammal, and see if you can draw the stages that they may have gone through to reach their present form and way of life.

Islands apart

Many islands have plants and animals that do not live anywhere else. Their ancestors were on the island when it broke away from the mainland or have swum, flown, or been carried on rafts to the island since. Once on the island, the animals and plants adapted to fill new or vacant niches.

MADAGASCAR

Africa

Madagascar

Madagascar is one of the most biodiverse islands on Earth. It split from Africa 165 million years ago. This was long before any of Africa's large mammals, such as elephants and giraffes had evolved, which is why they do not live there.

Good job I brought my rubber ring!

Hippos are thought to be the only large mammals to have swum to Madagascar.

Platypus

Cane toad

Echidna

Kangaroo

AUSTRALIA

Australia

This is home to two groups of special mammals. The monotremes comprise the echidnas and the platypus, and the marsupials include kangaroos, koalas, possums, bandicoots, and wombats.

My ambition is to be big in the Galápagos.

THE GALÁPAGOS

South America

Galápagos

Galápagos tortoises have grown huge because they have no predators.

These are a group of volcanic islands in the Pacific. They were never attached to the mainland, so all the species on them have arrived from somewhere else. Even though these islands have similar animals and plants, many have adapted to suit the local environment and are different from those on other islands. This is shown by differences in the beaks of finches and the shells and sizes of tortoises.

Sometimes evolution on islands is not all one way. Researchers in the Caribbean have found that Anolis lizards are washed into the sea during hurricanes and end up on a new island, where they breed with the local species. This mixes up the gene pool and slows down evolution. Other island animals, usually birds and bats, have returned to the mainland and evolved to suit their new home.

Anolis lizard

Madagascar is famous for its unique animals. These include primates (lemurs, sifakas, and aye-ayes), tenrecs, and chameleons. Since the island has been occupied by humans, many of the larger animals, such as the giant lemur, giant tortoises, pygmy hippo, and elephant bird, have died out. The rest are threatened by loss of habitat.

Ring-tailed lemur

Tenrec

Jackson's chameleon

Oi! Oz is over here, mate!

Although Australia is an island it is very close to the islands of Indonesia, which has allowed people and animals to cross. In some cases, the native animals and plants that had evolved to suit the local habitat have faced competition from invading species. The dingo replaced the Tasmanian tiger, which was hunted to extinction by humans, as the largest carnivore. Cane toads were introduced as a form of pest control in fields of sugar cane but are now pests themselves because they have no natural predators.

No way. I want to be in Amer-i-ca, plenty of trees in Amer-i-ca...

Some possums crossed to the New World before the continents split.

Dingo

Finches on the Galápagos have evolved different beaks that suit the type of food available on each island.

I'm only here for the sun, the sea, and the seaweed.

Marine iguanas have had to adapt to eating seaweed.

The Galápagos Islands

Same, *but different*

All life forms develop characteristics that suit where they live, what they eat, or how they move. This often results in species that look similar even though they are ***not related***. Take these five animals, for example...

armadillos *in N. America,* anteaters *in S. America,* aardvarks *and...*

What are the ants like in your part of the world?

Well, they're sort of tickly...

Bats and birds both fly, *but their wings*

It's really difficult to have a good scratch with these fingers.

Bats use a fast rowing motion to fly.

Wrist bones

Thumb

Fingers

It's a wing thing

It may have wings, but is it a bird? No – it could be a bat or an insect. Just because two animals have the same feature it doesn't mean they have a common ancestor. Sometimes things look the same because they have the same function. Birds and bats do not have a common winged ancestor so their wings show big differences.

Bats

Looking at this skeleton of a bat you can see its arm bones are very like those of a human. But instead of our own dainty digits it has oversized fingers that it uses to support the tough skin of the wing. Bats change the shape of their wings by flexing their fingers, which makes it easy for them to manoeuvre.

SIMILARITIES

- A flexible nose helps them root out insects.
- They have a long, sticky tongue that traps ants and termites. Anteaters can flick their tongue in and out 150 times a minute.
- They produce lots of saliva to keep the tongue sticky.
- All have strong claws for digging out ant hills.
- Aardvarks and armadillos have a few peg teeth, the rest have none.

pangolins in Africa,

and echidnas in Australia.

They get right up my nose, mate!

are not the same.

Large birds find it easier to glide than to keep flapping their wings.

Fingers

Wrist bones

Upper arm bone

Birds

Unlike flexible bat wings, a bird's wing is more rigid. Its upper arm bones are short and stiff, its wrist bones are fixed, and it has three tiny fingers. The feathers are supported by the arms, which makes it difficult to change direction quickly.

PARALLEL LINES

When unrelated species develop along similar lines to fill the same role in their environment it is called convergent evolution. Related species, such as porcupines in America and Africa, can also develop the same characteristics (in this case, quills) at the same time even though they have been physically separated for thousands of years. This process is sometimes called parallel evolution.

Poison dart frog

Mantella

Beware of the frog

South American poison dart frogs and the unrelated mantella frog of Madagascar have both developed a mechanism for storing poison from the ants that they eat in their skins. They have also developed bright skin colours as a warning.

Koala

Human

Finger of suspicion

Koalas are one of the few non-primates that have developed fingerprints. They are almost identical to human fingerprints, and each koala's prints are different. However, its closest relative, the wombat, doesn't have prints. Finger ridges help animals to grip things.

EmbryOs

EMBRYO: the early stage of an animal before it is born or hatches.

The embryos of many animals look very similar in the early stages of development. Some features will carry on growing to become limbs, teeth, or tails; others will vanish before the animal is born.

Limb buds

Spot the difference

Generally, embryos develop in an order that follows when each structure first evolved. The backbone is one of the earliest features to form in all vertebrates, with a head at one end and a tail at the other. Four limb buds then appear, as do the eyes. In the weeks that follow, the embryos become less alike as genes turn some things off and turn others on.

WHERE DID THAT COME FROM?

Every now and again an animal is born with an organ or structure that was common in one of its distant ancestors. Although it is of no use to the modern animal, its reappearance gives an indication of how genetic changes lead to new species.

On their toes

Modern horses have only one toe but their earliest ancestors had as many as five. Sometimes a foal is born with two tiny toes either side of the main hoof toe.

Tall tales

Stories of human babies being born with a short tail may seem unbelievable, but it happens. All humans have genes to grow tails but they usually get switched off early in development.

Claws on paws

Dogs have four toes on each foot. Sometimes an extra "dew" claw forms higher up on the back or front legs. They are often removed to prevent injury while exercising.

Flippin' amazing

Inside some whales and dolphins are small bones that show they once had back legs and that their ancestors walked on land. These occasionally reappear as tiny rear flippers.

Just when you think you don't need

Ernst Haeckel

Haeckel was a German biologist who drew a series of embryos in various stages of development to go with his theory that an animal embryo passes through stages resembling its adult evolutionary ancestors. It was later proved that embryos look like other closely related species rather than their ancestors.

SPOTS AND STRIPES

Whether an animal develops stripes or spots depends on two chemicals that interact to produce a pattern of spots in the skin of the embryo. These chemicals turn skin colour on or off and determine how big the spots will be. If there is too much of one of the chemicals the spots join up to form stripes. The size of the animal is also crucial — very small animals, such as mice, have no spots. In most large animals, such as elephants, the spots are very small and all blend together.

Spots form before stripes. So, spotted animals can have stripy tails, but stripy animals cannot have spotty tails because their spots have already spread into stripes.

HANGING AROUND

Many modern organisms have structures that had a practical use in their ancestors. Sometimes these have undergone a change of purpose, but more often they have become useless or have reached a point where they have only a limited function.

In a flap

Ostriches and emus have stumpy wings that can no longer be used to fly. Instead, the birds use them to balance themselves while running. They also flap them about in courtship displays.

Powerless flowers

Dandelions produce flowers and pollen, but neither of these is needed to produce seeds. The plant self-fertilizes to form seeds that will grow into clones of the parent plant.

Feeling their way

Moles and cave salamanders have eyes but do not use them. They have spent so long living in the dark that their eyes are useless for seeing anything other than light or shadow.

Hidden wings

Many species of earwigs have a pair of hindwings folded underneath leathery forewings. Earwigs rarely fly anywhere, even though they can — it takes them too long to unpack their wings.

something any more, it comes back!

Can *you* guess which of these are

We know that *humans* are related to CHIMPS and other members of the ape family. If we go back even further, we find we share ancestors with fish, *reptiles*, and insects. Ultimately, *every living thing* can trace

1 Hippo 2 Whale

Bear 3

Seal 4

5 Dog

Snake 6

7 Lizard

8 Dinosaur

Crocodile 9

Bird 10

ANSWERS

A hippo (1) is the whale's (2) closest living relative. Whales once had four legs and walked on land.

Bears (3), seals (4), and dogs (5) are closely related carnivores but are on a different branch of the evolutionary tree from cats and hyenas.

Some snakes (6) have hip bones, which shows they once had four legs like lizards (7), their close cousins.

Birds (10) evolved from dinosaurs (8), and both are descended from reptiles. The closest living reptilian relation of a bird is the crocodile (9).

CLOSE RELATIVES?

its ancestry to a **bacteria** that lived *billions of years ago*. Sometimes it's easy to spot family connections, but the LINKS AREN'T ALWAYS OBVIOUS. See if you can **work out** which of these are *close relatives*.

11 Cactus

12 Euphorbia

13 Spider crab

14 Horseshoe crab

Spider **15**

Elephant **16**

17 Dugong

Hyrax **18**

Wasp **20**

19 Hoverfly

Bumblebee **21**

Cacti (11) and euphorbias (12) are both desert plants but they are not related. They are an example of convergent evolution (see pages 76–77).

Dugongs (17) are the closest living relatives of the elephant (16) and they

Wasps (20) and bumblebees (21) are close relatives, but hoverflies (19) are not. They have evolved to look like wasps to deter predators.

Horseshoe crabs (14) are not really crabs and are more closely related to spiders (15) than to spider crabs (13).

are been related to the hyrax (18).

ANSWERS

Family trees

The horse family is often used as a classic example of how evolution works. There are plenty of horse fossils that show how minor changes occurred over millions of years. Some horses grew tall and then got smaller again, others kept three toes, while some rapidly diversified and equally quickly died out. They also show that many species of horse with different characteristics existed at the same time.

BRANCHING OUT

Evolution rarely follows a straight line from species to species. Instead it is more like a tree with many branches. Some of the branches lead on to new branches while others become dead ends. The horse family tree has many more branches than shown here, but this is the main route to the modern horse and its closest relatives. All the other species that evolved over millions of years have died out.

MODERN HORSE

All living horses are descended from Old World stock, since American horses went extinct as the ice ages began. They include zebras, asses, onagers, and kiangs.

Equus caballus, the modern domestic horse

EQUUS

The first modern horses were the height of a donkey. They had a long neck and legs, a flexible muzzle, and a deep jaw. Their teeth were straight and crested for grazing. They spread rapidly and diversified throughout the Old and New Worlds.

4 million years ago

One-toed hoof strengthens to prevent

RECENT 2.6 MYA–PRESENT

PLIOCENE 5.3–2.6 MYA

PLIOHIPPUS

This was once thought to be a direct ancestor of *Equus*. *Pliohippus* gradually lost its side toes and ran on a single hoof, but its teeth were curved and its face was different from modern horses.

MERYCHIPPUS

These animals still had three toes but stood on tiptoe for faster running. The centre toe was starting to develop into a hoof. The muzzle looked more horse-like.

QUAGGA RETURNS

The quagga is a subspecies of the plains zebra that was wiped out in the 1870s. It differed from other zebras by having stripes only on its neck and head while the rest of its body was brown. Using DNA from a stuffed quagga, scientists worked out its genetic code. Attempts are now being made to re-create it through selective breeding from existing zebras that have fewer stripes and brownish coats.

MIOHIPPUS

These horses had longer legs and three toes front and back. The face grew longer and the teeth began to adapt to eating tough grass.

HYRACOTHERIUM

The ancestor of the horse was the size of a dog. It had four toes on its front feet and three on the back, and had pads rather than hooves. Its teeth show it ate soft leaves.

15 million years ago

Side bones reduce to leave a central hoof.

17 million years ago

Foot becomes adapted for running on hard ground.

36 million years ago

Three toes touched the ground, but still had pads.

55 million years ago

All horses began as an animal with four front toes.

MIOCENE 23–5.3 MYA

OLIGOCENE 34–23 MYA

EOCENE 55–34 MYA (MILLION YEARS AGO)

How the *elephant*

The elephant's trunk is an amazing example of evolutionary development. It is in fact a combined nose and upper lip that lengthened as the elephant's ancestors became taller and their tusks grew bigger. With such a heavy head, you need an easy way to touch the ground.

Can *your* nose do this?

MOERITHERIUM

This semi-aquatic animal was small and had a long, mobile upper lip. It had enlarged incisor teeth, but these had not yet grown into tusks.

PHIOMIA

Phiomia had a short trunk formed from the nose and the upper lip. It also had short upper and lower tusks, and a long bottom lip.

PALAEOMASTODON

Palaeomastodon is believed to be the first ancestor of the elephant line. *Moeritherium* and *Phiomia* are thought to be early side branches on the evolutionary tree.

GOMPHOTHERIUM

The gomphotheres had four tusks, the bottom two set into a shovel-like lower jaw. The trunk began to lengthen to help them feed and drink as the animals grew taller.

PRIMELEPHAS

Primelephas was the ancestor of all modern elephants. It had smaller bottom tusks and a longer trunk than *Gomphotherium*.

Mastodons had cone-shaped teeth that were used to crush twigs and leaves from shrubs and trees. They lived near swamps and woodlands and may have used their tusks to knock trees over.

34 million years ago

23 million years ago

Eocene   Oligocene   Miocene

84

got his *trunk*

Asian elephants have only one lobe at the tip of their trunks so they have to wrap the trunk around objects to pick them up.

In Kipling's *Just So* story, the elephant went to the river for a drink. A crocodile grabbed his nose, which got longer and longer as he tried to pull free.

Mammoths were not as big as you may think – they were the same size as modern elephants, but had longer tusks and a high-domed head and shoulders. The trunk reached to the ground and had two flexible lobes at the end for grasping leaves.

MAMMOTH

ANANCUS

The teeth of mammoths and modern elephants evolved into a series of hard ridges that were better adapted to grinding up tough grasses.

Asian elephants are more closely related to mammoths than African elephants. They too have a slightly domed head but it is only the males that have tusks. The tip of an elephant's trunk is highly sensitive. It is not only used for breathing but also for sucking up water. The trunk can pick up objects and be waved aggressively.

ASIAN ELEPHANT

AFRICAN ELEPHANT

Mastodons were an early offshoot of the evolutionary tree. They had lost their lower tusks but the top ones were long and curved. They had a low-domed head and a shaggy coat.

MASTODON

STEGODON

African elephants have a flattened head and both sexes have tusks. Their trunks end in two lobes, which they can pinch together to pick up tiny objects.

5.3 million years ago

2.6 million years ago

10,000 years ago

Pliocene

Pleistocene

Today

RELATIVE FACTS

From ape *to human*

Out of Africa

Darwin's idea that man was descended from the apes and came out of Africa upset many people. At that time there was little evidence – only a few Neanderthal skulls and bones had been found. Later, the bones of an early ape and the first example of *Homo erectus*, an early hominin from Java, were discovered. These were followed by examples of *Homo sapiens* dating back 30,000 years from Europe and Indonesia. It wasn't until 1967 that older fossils of *Homo sapiens* were discovered in Ethiopia. These have been dated back 195,000 years, proving that Darwin was correct.

Human evolution is the most remarkable of any mammal. No other species has developed as fast or colonized as much of the world as we have. Modern man, *Homo sapiens*, is the last of a series of human-like creatures that we call hominins. Our early ancestors were small and ape-like. They walked on two feet but bent their knees and hips. They ate leaves and fruit, but left the forest to search for other foods out on the savanna. As the diet changed, stronger teeth and jaws were required,

It all began when I started walking upright and moved out of the forest...

I've got the hang of walking, but I still can't run. Physically, I'm taller and stronger, and I'm going places.

PARANTHROPUS (P.) AETHIOPICUS

ARDIPITHECUS RAMIDUS

AUSTRALOPITHECUS (A.) ANAMENSIS

A. AFARENSIS

A. AFRICANUS

HOMO (H.) RUDOLFENSIS

Human evolution has taken 5 million years. Many

Hands and feet

Most primates can stand on two feet, but only humans stay upright all the time. It is thought that early humans may have had to forage over long distances to find food during a dry period in history, and walking was a more efficient way to travel. Standing up also freed the hands to carry food and use them for throwing things and handling tools. Because evolution of a thumb allowed us to touch each of the other fingers, humans can grip and manipulate objects easily.

Lack of hair

Humans have very little hair compared with other primates. It is thought we may have evolved this feature because:

1. it made it easier to forage for food in shallow water

2. it helped us lose heat faster on the hot savannas

3. it helped to reduce numbers of parasites on the body.

Luckily, humans learned to catch animals and used their skins to keep warm at night.

which gradually changed the shape of the face and skull. It is thought that the australopithecines were the ancestors of the earliest species of *Homo*. This new branch of upright hominins developed an advantage by using tools and hunting for meat. Improvements in the diet led to increases in brain size and abilities. They developed language, began to live in communities, and worked together in groups. *Homo sapiens* emerged 250,000 years ago, and you are a descendant.

RELATIVE FACTS

Hobbits

The discovery of very small hominin fossils has led to debate about whether this is a new species, *Homo floresiensis,* or a human population that suffered from dwarfism. If it is a new species then it is the longest lasting non-modern human, having died out only about 12,000 years ago.

Your inner fish

The fact that humans hiccup may date back to our watery ancestors. Wiring in the brain that pushes water over fish gills and makes amphibians gulp air has been imperfectly re-wired in mammals. It can make the diaphragm go into spasm, causing hiccups.

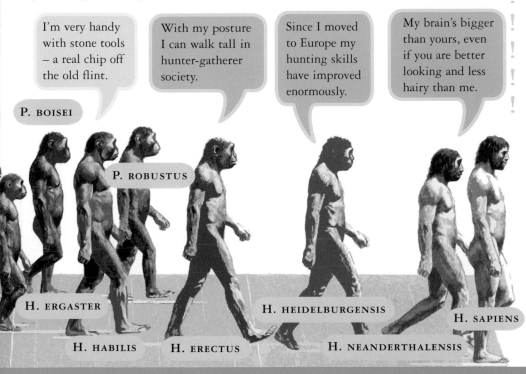

I'm very handy with stone tools – a real chip off the old flint.

With my posture I can walk tall in hunter-gatherer society.

Since I moved to Europe my hunting skills have improved enormously.

My brain's bigger than yours, even if you are better looking and less hairy than me.

P. BOISEI

P. ROBUSTUS

H. ERGASTER

H. HABILIS

H. ERECTUS

H. HEIDELBURGENSIS

H. NEANDERTHALENSIS

H. SAPIENS

species went before us, but we are the only one left.

Increasing brain size

One of the most significant human evolution trends was the increase in brain size from 400 cm³ (24 in³) to around 1,400 cm³ (85 in³) today. Scientists think that as our diet improved, including more protein, fat, and better carbohydrates, this provided more energy for brain function so the brain could grow, which in turn led to greater intelligence and skills.

It's the wrinkly bits of my brain that give me my social skills, working memory, language, and sensory abilities.

The human brain may have grown, but the skull hasn't. The brain has had to fold itself up to fit in.

Brain size gradually increased as we progressed from an ape to a modern human.

HUMAN *behaviour*

Why do we behave the way we do? While it's obvious that our bodies have evolved physically, our minds have also made great evolutionary leaps. However, there are still many things we do instinctively that have their origins in the past.

Start here

One of the main differences between humans and other animals is language. Our ability to communicate began with simple hand gestures and sounds that represented specific things. Gradually we began to combine these to express ideas that were impossible with single words. As patterns developed in how words were used, they became the rules of grammar. This allows us to express any number of ideas with a limited set of words.

FACIAL EXPRESSIONS

We pull faces every day, often without realizing we're doing it. They convey distinct meanings without the need for words. Some evolved as a way to express feelings and change other people's reactions to us. Others, like disgust, are a physical reaction to a particular stimulus.

HAPPINESS   **SADNESS**   **ANGER**   **FEAR**

Many *facial expressions*

Hunters v. Gatherers

Many male and female behaviours date back to our hunter-gatherer ancestors where men brought home the mammoth steaks and women looked after the cave and the kids. This is probably why men can read maps and women like shopping – it's all down to our days on the savanna.

 Hunters had to remember points in the landscape (hence mapreading skills).

 Gatherers searched for the best fruit bushes (a bit like shopping).

 Aggression came from defending territory, confronting wild animals, and waging war.

 Caring instinct developed from bringing up young and looking after the rest of the tribe.

Better at running, jumping, throwing, and catching mammoths.

Better at handling small objects and remembering where things are.

Like to compete against each other, and in teams against rival tribes.

Prefer to get on with everybody for tribal harmony and cooperation.

View relationships with others in terms of hierarchy (who is top dog).

 View relationships in terms of family, emotional, and social bonds.

 Communicate as a means to solve problems and to establish rank.

 Communicate to establish social connections and intimacy.

Prefer to play games that have fixed rules, are competitive, and end with winners and losers.

 Prefer to play games where all players do the same thing, such as skating or riding.

Baby talk

All babies have an inborn ability to learn language. They pick up words simply by listening to people around them. As they get older, the patterns of a language get fixed into their brains. Adults often find it hard to learn new languages because it is difficult to fix new patterns of grammar in an already "hard-wired" brain.

DISGUST   SURPRISE   INTEREST

are universal.

Humour

All humans instinctively laugh, but how do we recognize a joke? One possibility is that our brain recognizes a pattern and is surprised by it. Babies laugh at games that involve surprises, such as peekaboo, before they learn to talk. As we get older we start recognizing patterns in language. Jokes are just surprising uses of language we respond to by laughing.

 Peepo!

Surviving sickness

For all our brain power, physical ability, and sheer ingenuity, the human body is far from perfect. It can be attacked by invading organisms, has bits we don't need, and mechanisms that work too well. So why, despite all our other evolutionary advances, are we still so vulnerable to disease?

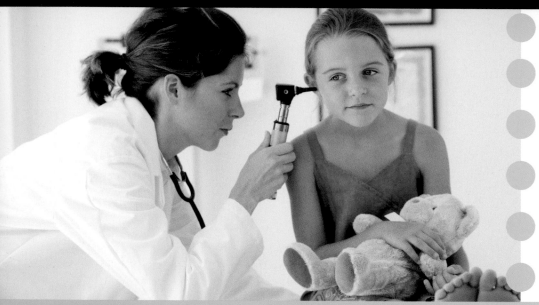

Back to nature

All living things get sick, and humans are no different. Many doctors are now looking at how evolution has shaped the human body and its systems and why it has left us with so many problems. Illnesses can be caused by faulty genes, invading bugs, design defects, and our own defence mechanisms. We are also facing new problems that nature hasn't had time to deal with. Examining our past may help us to have a healthier future.

Upsides and downsides

Sickle-cell anaemia is a common disease. It affects red blood cells, bending them into a rigid shape that makes them get stuck in blood vessels. People who inherit a copy of the sickle-cell gene from each parent suffer painful attacks and tend to die young. However, people who have one or both of the genes are resistant to malaria, which kills many people in hot countries. People without sickle cell genes are more likely to get malaria, so even though it causes disease, sickle cell has benefits and that is why the gene survives.

Defence mechanisms

Why do we cough? We do it to clear our lungs. Without coughing we would not be able to get rid of irritants that might lead to choking or lung infections. Many of the things we think of as symptoms are useful in helping the body fight disease. Fever is a deliberate rise in body temperature that helps kill viruses and bacteria. When you vomit you get rid of poisons that could upset the body's systems.

Leftovers

The appendix is a little piece of intestine that seems to have no useful purpose. In theory, evolution should have got rid of it ages ago, because if it becomes infected it can kill us. Doctors now think it may be a place where gut bacteria hide during a bout of diarrhoea. Its size seems to be crucial. A small, thin appendix is more likely to become inflamed, so selection may be favouring large appendixes.

I'm going to have to run around the park to work this off.

Too much fat

Back when man was a hunter-gatherer, foods containing fat and sugar were rare in the diet. People who could eat large amounts of these foods and put weight on quickly had an advantage in surviving famines. Today these foods are plentiful, but we still have the urge to eat as much of them as possible. Humans now face problems with obesity, diabetes, and heart disease because we don't do enough exercise to burn up the excess fat and sugar.

Beating the bugs

Many diseases in humans are caused by bacteria. Natural selection favours the bacteria because they can reproduce every 15 minutes and evolve to a new strain in as little as a day. Antibiotics have helped us fight infections but have also helped the bacteria by killing off weaker strains. This has left us with drug-resistant varieties that are extremely difficult to control.

Atchoo!

Our immune system is a mechanism that has evolved to combat **invading organisms.** It produces molecules called antibodies that stick to an invader so that IT CAN BE ENGULFED by a white blood cell. Sometimes the system goes into *overdrive,* producing an extreme allergic reaction to harmless things such as POLLEN or peanuts. This can be *highly dangerous.* Scientists hope to design a drug that can prevent these reactions from becoming **fatal.**

Sneezing is an allergic response. It can blast irritants out of the body at 160 kph (100 mph).

still evolving

Evolution for complex life forms is an incredibly slow process and it is very hard to see it in action.

CHANGE FOR THE BETTER?

Physically, the human body seems to have changed very little in the last 50,000 years in how it looks and functions. However, improvements in diet and easy availability of food in the developed world have led to us becoming taller and fatter than our recent ancestors. Humans are also living longer and there are more of us, so the gene pool

It may take **thousands** of *generations* before every

Genetic selection

New technology may have a more rapid effect on human evolution by allowing humans to choose what features their children are born with, such as intelligence or hair colour. This could create ethical problems over whether we should try to eliminate "undesirable" traits, such as aggression or hereditary disease, or keep them in the gene pool.

I'd like a girl with blue eyes and brown hair, please.

Special powers

We don't have any superheroes who can fly or see through brick walls without mechanical help, but could it happen one day? It would take a lot of changes in our genes before humans could fly. It is impossible to reintroduce a trait once the genes have been lost, and our last ancestor with wing potential went on to become a bat rather than Batman.

Genetic changes are highly unpredictable and happen in response to changes in our environment. Scientists are divided about whether humans are still evolving or if we have reached our biological peak. Who knows where we might go from here?

is acquiring mutations faster than ever. But now that we have more control over our environment other things may start to drive evolutionary change. We can now use biotechnology to change our genes, so our future may be in our own hands.

member of a **population** shows a favourable *adaptation*.

The ultimate upload

One possible route science may take us along is a merger of man and technology. We already use bionics to replace defective limbs and organs. It may one day be possible to implant chips in the brain that make up for loss of speech or vision, or allow us to do things we're not good at. Imagine uploading a new learning programme instead of doing homework!

Yeah man, this low gravity is stretching me to the limit.

Life on other planets

Another way humans might take a new evolutionary path is if we colonize other planets. Colonizers would face new environmental conditions, such as low gravity or lack of oxygen, that require new adaptations. Over centuries the colonizers (and any animals and plants that they took with them) would evolve to look, think, and behave differently.

GLOSSARY

Adaptation an inherited feature of a living thing that helps it to survive and reproduce in its environment.

Amphibian an animal, such as a frog or newt. Most need water in which to lay their eggs.

Ancestor an individual who lived in the past from whom other individuals have descended.

Arthropods invertebrate animals with a hard external skeleton and paired jointed legs. They include insects and crustaceans.

Artificial selection the process of selectively breeding plants and animals over time.

Australopithecine an early form of human that lived in Africa.

Bacteria microscopic single-celled organisms, some of which cause disease.

Biodiversity the number and variety of species living in a specific area or region.

Biotechnology the science of altering an organism's genes.

Botanist a person who studies plants.

Carnivore an animal that eats mainly meat.

Cell one of the microscopic structures that make up living things. Cells normally have an outer membrane, a jelly-like filling, and a nucleus in the middle.

Characteristics the many variations of a gene.

Chromosome a thread-like structure in a cell's nucleus that contains DNA.

Classification the organization of different living things into related groups.

Common ancestor the most recent species from which two different species evolved.

Convergent evolution the process where organisms that are not related independently evolve similar traits as a result of having to adapt to a similar environment.

Crinoid an ancient group of invertebrates that includes sea lilies and feather stars that still exists today.

Cycad a palm-tree-like plant.

DNA deoxyribonucleic acid, a very long double helix-shaped molecule (group of atoms) that carries genetic information as a chemical code.

Diversification a process of increasing variation among organisms that may lead to the development of new species.

Dominant gene a gene that has priority over a recessive (weaker) gene.

Embryo an organism in its early stages of development.

Evolution the process of change over time that occurs due to natural selection.

Extinction the disappearance of a species or a population.

Fertilization the fusion of male and female sex cells to create an embryo.

Fossils remains or traces of long-dead plants and animals that have been preserved in rock.

Gene a section of inherited code in DNA, which, when switched on, causes a specific reaction in a cell.

Gene flow the spread of genes from one population to another by migration and interbreeding.

Gene pool the total of all the genetic variations of a population.

Generation a group of individuals born and living at the same time.

Genetic bottleneck loss of genetic variations caused by a dramatic reduction in a species' population.

Genetic drift random changes in the frequency of traits in a population that occur by chance; one of the processes that drives evolution.

Genetics the study of genes and their effects.

Genetic variation the variety of genes present in a population through inheritance of genetic material.

Genome all the genetic information of a living thing.

Geologist a person who studies the origin and structure of Earth and its rock formations.

Habitat the area or environment in which an organism lives.

Hominin name for the evolutionary line, including the australopithecines, that led to modern humans, after they split off from chimpanzees and apes.

Hunter-gatherer description of how our early ancestors lived by hunting for animals and gathering fruit, seeds, and other plant material for eating.

Hybrid offspring produced by the breeding between individuals from different species.

Immune system the body's defence against invading organisms and foreign substances.

Invertebrate an animal that does not have a backbone.

Marsupial a group of mammals that give birth to underdeveloped young, which they then carry in a pouch. Kangaroos and koalas are marsupials.

Mollusc an invertebrate animal that has a soft body and often a hard outer shell. Snails and clams are molluscs.

Mutation a sudden change to a gene that results in genetic variation if inherited. The change can have either no effect, a harmful effect, or a helpful effect.

Natural selection the theory proposed by Darwin that is one of the processes causing evolution; individuals with the most favourable characteristics are more likely to survive.

Naturalist a person who studies plants and animals.

Neanderthal a recent hominin that lived at the same time as modern man, but who disappeared 25,000 years ago.

New World the continent of North and South America.

Niche the space and role occupied by an organism in an environment.

Nocturnal describes an animal that is active at night.

Nucleic acid a long, complex organic molecule such as DNA.

Old World the continents of Europe, Asia, and Africa.

Organism a living thing.

Ozone a toxic type of oxygen molecule that forms a layer in the atmosphere and prevents harmful radiation from reaching Earth.

Pangaea a supercontinent of all Earth's landmasses that formed in the late Permian and began to split apart in the Jurassic.

Parallel evolution where two related species evolve similar traits at the same time even though they are geographically separated.

Period a division of geological time. Each is given a name, such as Cambrian, Silurian, Triassic, Jurassic, and so on.

Pollination the transfer of pollen from the male part to the female part of a flower.

Population a group of individuals of the same species.

Predator an animal that hunts and feeds on another.

Primates the group of mammals that includes apes and humans.

Primitive describes an early undeveloped characteristic seen in an ancestor.

Pterosaur an extinct flying reptile with featherless membrane wings.

Recessive gene a gene that is only expressed in the absence of a dominant gene.

Reproduction the production of offspring during which genes are passed on from the parent or parents.

Reptile an animal that crawls on its belly or walks on short legs and whose skin is covered in bony plates or scales. Lizards are reptiles.

Sauropod a four-legged, plant-eating dinosaur that had a small head and a long neck and tail. Brachiosaurs were sauropods.

Savanna a tropical grassland with drought-resistant plants (mainly grasses) and few trees.

Sexual selection a form of natural selection where an individual selects a mate with a preferred characteristic.

Speciation the formation of a new species.

Species a group of related organisms that are capable of interbreeding to produce fertile offspring.

Subspecies a local population of a species that has slight genetic differences to the parent species but can still interbreed with it.

Tetrapod a land-walking vertebrate animal that has four limbs.

Trait a feature determined by a gene or a group of genes.

Trilobite a type of ancient marine arthropod.

Variation a difference in the structural or functional characteristics of an organism that is not seen in the rest of the species or population.

Vertebrate an animal that has a backbone.

Zoologist a person who studies animals and their behaviour.

INDEX

Acknowledgements

Dorling Kindersley would like to thank Penny Smith for editorial help with this book and Peter Bull for the illustrations on pages 72 and 73.

The publisher would like to thank the following for their kind permission to reproduce their photographs:

(Key: a-above; b-below/bottom; c-centre; f-far; l-left; r-right; t-top)

akg-images: Erich Lessing 10cra; **Alamy Images:** APIX 30b; Arco Images / W. Dolder 81bl (hyrax); Erwan Balanca / Jupiterimages / Stock Image 31tr; David Ball 24cb; Peter Barritt 52cra; birdpix 52c; blickwinkel 49bl; Brandon Cole Marine Photography 35br; Nigel Cattlin 58-59; David Chapman 53cr; FLPA 53fbl; Chris Fredriksson 48cr; Bob Gibbons 29bc; Nick Greaves 77cla; Tim Hill 28tr; David Hosking 48c; Interfoto Pressebildagentur 12cla; Janine Wiedel Photolibrary 40bl; Piotr & Irena Kolasa 79clb; Dennis Kunkel / Phototake Inc. 90cl; Lebrecht Music and Arts Photo Library 5cla, 21cb, 24cla; The London Art Archive 13cr, 19cb, 25crb, 36crb; Celia Mannings 74br; Mary Evans Picture Library 11b, 15tl, 17bl, 20bc, 30tr, 38 (Emma Darwin), 38bca, 42clb, 43tr; moodboard 60tr; Keith Morris 91br; Tsuneo Nakamura / Volvox Inc. 34-35b (water); Natural History Museum, London 36clb; The Natural History Museum 24tl, 83br; Nature Alan King 67cla; North Wind Picture Archives 23tc, 38c (Darwin); Old Paper Studios 38-39t (piano); Ian Paterson 10cla; Paul Thompson Images 53cra; Miguel Angel Muñoz Pellicer 12cra; Photodisc Inc. 66c; The Print Collector 15cr, 20br, 27cr, 30cra (Malthus), 72bl; Robert Harding Picture Library Ltd 54cr; David J. Slater 53br; David Tipling 32cr; Jeff Tucker 27cl; Rob Walls 18cl; Dave Watts 73cra; WorldFoto 77cra; **Ardea:** Chris Harvey 59tr; Steve Hopkin 58ca, 58cb; **The Art Archive:** Gemaldegalerie, Dresden 11t; **Auckland Museum:** 25cl; **British Library:** 85tl; **Corbis:** Heide Benser / zefa 47br (freckles); K. & H. Benser / zefa 74bl, 75clb, 75crb (rafts); Tom Brakefield 76ca; Tim Davis / Davis Lynn Wildlife 11cl; Nigel J. Dennis / Gallo Images 76cra; DLILLC / Davis Lynn Wildlife 48br; Historical Picture Archive 17ca; Images.com 92br; Peter Johnson 75ca (tenrec); Frans Lanting 2fcrb, 3clb (*Psilotum nudum*), 65bl, 68cr; Joe McDonald 76cla; moodboard 61crb; Arthur Morris 77clb; Jim Richardson 61tr; Galen Rowell 75br; Staffan Widstrand 77ca; **Reproduced with permission from John**

van Wyhe ed., The Complete Work of Charles Darwin Online (http://darwin-online.org.uk/): 6 (sidebar), 6bc, 6br, 6ftr, 6t (frogs), 6tl, 6tl (fish), 6-7bc, 7 (sidebar), 7bc, 7br, 7ftl, 7ftr, 7tl, 7tr, 15br, 16bl (book, 16tl, 17bc (chimp), 17bc (expressions), 17br, 18bc, 18tl, 19 (moths), 19tl, 20, 22b (chart), 22ca (Beagle), 22-23bc, 23br, 23cl, 23tl, 23tr, 25cr, 30-31 (b/w frogs), 37cr (insert), 37crb, 54cl, 72-73 (diagram background), 94br, 94cl, 94crb, 94fcra, 94tr, 95bl, 95br, 95cra, 95fbl, 95tl; **DK Images:** Booth Museum of Natural History, Brighton 74fcl (platypus); Philip Dowell 79tr; Hunterian Museum and Art Gallery, University of Glasgow 69ca; London Butterfly House, Syon Park 21t (butterflies), 95cb; Sonia Moore 27b (boxes); Natural History Museum, London 3clb, 5tl, 14cb, 15clb, 25bl, 33cb (bumble bee), 71bc, 78clb, 84cla, 84clb, 84cra, 84crb, 85cla, 96tl; Oxford University Museum of Natural History 31tl; Rough Guides 10l (vegetation); Royal Geographical Society, London 18tr; The Science Museum, London 19cla, 21l (flask), 96tc; The Home of Charles Darwin, Down House (English Heritage) 26tl; The Home of Charles Darwin, Down House (English Heritage) / Natural History Museum, London 22clb; Barrie Watts 53bl; Jerry Young 74fclb (echidna); **Reprinted with permission from Encyclopædia Britannica, © 2005 by Encyclopædia Britannica, Inc.:** 55 (finches); **The English Heritage Photo Library:** 18c, 26cl; By kind permission of Darwin Heirlooms Trust 20tr; **Getty Images:** American Images Inc. 47c (dimples); Torbjorn Arvidson / Nordic Photos 60b; The Bridgeman Art Library 8-9, 9bl (monkey), 14-15b, 22cl, 22tr, 22-23c (sea), 33tl; Alice Edward / Stone 34tl (jar); Jamie Grill / Iconica 90cla; Hulton Archive 20crb; Jeff Hunter / Photographer's Choice 60ca; John Lamb / Stone 61tl; Régine Mahaux / Riser 10br (man); Mark Moffett / Minden Pictures 54br; Jeff Sherman 93bl; Scott Sroka / National Geographic 63br; ZSSD / Minden Pictures 50cb; **Matthew Harris / John F. Fallon at the University of Wisconsin-Madison:** 62bl; **iStockphoto.com:** Roman Kobzarev 32c; Alexandre Zveiger 47bl (hand); **Courtesy Thomas J. Lemieux:** 73tl; **Mary Evans Picture Library:** 16b (Huxley), 16b (Wilberforce), 16cr, 21bl, 21c; **Sean McCann:** 79bc; **National Library Of Scotland:** Reproduced with permission of the Trustees of the National Library of Scotland 16cl; **The Natural History Museum, London:** 23bc, 26bl, 26crb, 26tr, 27cla, 27cra, 67tc; **PA Photos:** Barry Batchelor / PA Archive 51bl; **Dr Andrew Pask:** 63ca; **Photolibrary:** Nicholas Eveleigh / Digital Vision 26-27c, 84-85b; Nick Koudis / Photodisc 47fbr; Oxford Scientific (OSF) / Carlos Sanchez Alonso 53cl; Photodisc 37; PureStock 77fcra; Stockbyte 91tl; **Photoshot:** Mark Fairhurst / UPPA 27fcl; **Science Photo Library:** 15cra, 51tl; Michael Abbey 67cl; Mauricio

Anton 87tr; Sally Bensusen 69br; Annabella Bluesky 47cl; Tony Camacho 50bl; Michael Clutson 49cb; Ted Clutter 70cl; CNRI 49ca; Lynette Cook 66ftl, 67cr; Darwin Dale 58crb; Christian Darkin 70bl, 83bc, 83c; Dept. Of Clinical Cytogenetics, Addenbrookes Hospital 47cl, 47crb, 47fclb, 47fcrb; Georgette Douwma 34bl, 66cr; Pascal Goetgheluck 86tl, 87bl (skulls); Patrick Lynch 34fbl; Dr P. Marazzi 50br; Tom Mchugh 34br; Mark Miller 87crb (brain); Dr G. Moscoso 64tl; Pasieka 44crb; Raul Gonzalez Perez 34tl, 34tl (eye balls); Philippe Plailly / Eurelios 3bc (modern man), 71fcrb; Philippe Psaila 45clb; Nemo Ramjet 3br, 93bc; James H. Robinson 50c; P. Rona / OAR / National Undersea Research Program / NOAA 66fl; Kaj R. Svensson 68c; Joe Tucciarone 2tl, 70cb; Lena Untidt / Bonnier Publications 58cra; L. Willatt, East Anglian Regional Genetics Service 43bc; **Shutterstock:** 36-37b; alle 59tl; Nick Biemans 45bc; Bryan Busovicki 39bc; Cheryl Casey 47fbl; Chiyacat 29ca; Paul Cowan 28cra; John de la Bastide 29b; Adem Demir 41tl; Miodrag Gajic 51crb; garloon 38cra (trumpet); János Gehring 72-73 (background); Gelpi 64cl; Angelo Gilardelli 41bl; GoodMood Photo 24r; Eric Isselée 5clb, 40tr; javarman 12cra (books); Adrian T. Jones 32cl; Sebastian Kaulitzki 40cl; Christopher King 36l; Oleg Kozlov, Sophy Kozlova 45crb; Kudryashka 76-77 (globes); Timur Kulgarin 18bl; Sergey Lavrentev 45cb; LiveStock 88-89b; Maugli 25; Najin 75t (paper); Andrei Nekrassov 34fbr; Donald P. Oehman 39clb; Kirsty Pargeter 40crb; Thomas M. Perkins 90bl; Florin Tirlea 24r (pile); Irina Tischenko 45br; Shachar Weis 29br; **Still Pictures:** BIOS, François Gilson 31br; **SuperStock:** Jaime Abecasis 9br; **University of Calgary:** Ken Bendiktsen / Jason Anderson 72crb; **University of Chicago.** Model by Tyler Keillor, photo by Beth Rooney: 72cr (Tiktaalik).

Jacket images: Front: DK Images: The National Birds of Prey Centre, Gloucestershire clb (eagle); Natural History Museum, London tl (*Phiomia*); Jerry Young bc (crocodile); fbl (leopard); **Getty Images:** Zubin Shroff / Stone+ b (background); **PunchStock:** Digital Vision / Y. Taro c. **Back: Reproduced with permission from John van Wyhe ed., The Complete Work of Charles Darwin Online** (http://darwin-online.org.uk/): cla, tl; **Science Photo Library:** Kaj R. Svensson br.

All other images © Dorling Kindersley. For further information see: www.dkimages.com